# Fashion With Ribbon

# Fashion With Ribbon

### Kay Anderson

B.T. Batsford Ltd · London

© Kay Anderson 1987
First published 1987

All rights reserved. No part of this publication
may be reproduced, in any form or by any means,
without permission from the Publisher.

ISBN 0 7134 5228 5

Typeset by Tek-Art Ltd, Kent
and printed in Great Britain by
Anchor Brendon Ltd
Tiptree, Essex
for the publishers
B.T. Batsford Ltd
4 Fitzhardinge Street
London W1H 0AH

# CONTENTS

# DEDICATION

To my sister Barbara

# ACKNOWLEDGEMENTS

I would like to thank most sincerely:

**Selectus Ltd.** for their generosity and help, and for supplying all the beautiful Panda ribbons used in this book and
**Newey Goodman Ltd.** for their generous support and help.

My thanks also to the following:
The Fashion Research Centre; Museum of Costume, Bath; the Embroiderers' Guild, Hampton Court; and the Herbert Art Gallery, Coventry, for help in preparing the history of the ribbon weaving industry; the Vilene organization for kindly supplying all the interfacings.

Stewart Downie for all the photography, with the exception of colour plates 6, 7, 17 (Matt Mathias) and colour plates 3, 4 (Brian Wootton); to my models: Helen Fairbrother, Barbara and Jennie Parker, Elaine Londesborough and Nicola Blackburn; to my students for allowing their work to be photographed: Barbara Parker (picture 13), Dorothy Thomason (picture 54) and Julie Green (picture 24); to Ann Olphin for her ribbon rose picture (colour plate 22); Christine Kingdom for introducing me to ribbon weaving. All the other work featured in this book has been designed and made by the author. Richard Chung for his excellent interpretation of the various weaving patterns; Kay Sweeney for helping with the illustrations of my design; Jean Green and Shirley Londesborough for patiently typing my manuscript; for lots of practical help; Diana Lewis and Linda Hamilton; and Shirley Woolley for her constant and constructive encouragement.

And finally, my family: My eldest son Stephen for all his help with the work on the table setting. Christina and Andrew for all their help weaving the ribbons for the bed quilt. Paul for all his meticulous help with the time-consuming graphics, and my husband Alec for his infinite patience and support at all times.

# INTRODUCTION

Designer clothes are usually recognized by the beautiful quality fabrics and trimmings used. In addition, a large amount of hand-sewing or decorative work goes into them, which makes them expensive and out of reach of a great many people.

*Fashion with ribbon* is intended to inspire you to create your own 'designer' look and finish, to clothes and accessories, using one of the most versatile and readily available materials for this purpose.

The beautiful but practical ribbons we can buy today have evolved from an industry with a surprisingly long and and important history. Ribbon weaving was first reported in France in the mid-fourteenth century when women wove dress trimmings and sashes. Ribbon production gradually developed in certain areas; Paris, Lyons and St. Etienne (France), Krefeld (Germany), Basle (Switzerland), Vienna (Austria) and Coventry (England). During the eighteenth century, France was already exporting ribbons to England, mainly from St. Etienne, where the weavers produced brilliant designs of richly ornamented ribbons entwined with silver and gold lamé in the silk threads. Producing these ribbons was very costly, as the machinery was extremely complex and it took several weeks to set up a loom before weaving could begin, but the early ribbon manufacturers were painstaking in their work and meticulous with their products, which were as rich as any hand embroidery. Other centres of the trade worked for a restricted market only. In the nineteenth century, ribbon industries grew in Paterson (U.S.A.), Moscow, Belgium and Spain. The competition became intense, the largest exporters being St. Etienne and Basle. The beautiful jacquard ribbons made in St. Etienne were exported to England, Germany, Belgium, Brazil, Chile, Mexico and Spain. St. Etienne, however, imported plain ribbons from Basle, which were the speciality of that city. At the London exhibition in 1851, several prizes were awarded to the Basle weavers.

Coventry began silk ribbon weaving in the late seventeenth century, with the advent of the Hugenots, the Protestant refugees fleeing from the French silk-weaving area. At first, only plain ribbons were made, but such were the skills of these weavers that Coventry began to dominate the fancy end of the ribbon market and in the eighteenth century the city and the area to the north became the most important centre for their manufacture in Britain.

Coventry, during early Victorian times, was unique in its dependence on the ribbon industry, as a quarter of its population were employed as ribbon weavers. It was in fact the nineteenth century that enjoyed the greatest prosperity for the ribbon weavers, when the industry achieved worldwide importance.

Until the advent of steam, the mainstay of the ribbon industry was the outworker. The weavers collected the silk from the manufacturers and wove the ribbons in a room in their houses. This room was known as the topshop and these were attached to the houses of the master weavers who were called 'first hands'.

However, following the introduction of steam, factories were established in Coventry. To compete with these, the master weavers added steam power to their topshops, thus creating small cottage factories. This was considered unique in Europe. For many years there was remarkable harmony between manufacturers and weavers in Coventry, but during 1856 and 1860 this relationship deteriorated, partly due to dispute over list prices paid to the weavers, and partly due to a commercial treaty between France and England in 1860 establishing free trade. This resulted in lockouts, strikes and great hardship to many thousands of weavers and their families. Many skilled weavers emigrated to the U.S.A., Canada, Australia and New Zealand.

From the mid-1830's to 1860 the Coventry ribbon manufacturers enjoyed prosperity and progress, owing mainly to the introduction of a loom designed by Joseph Marie Jacquard (1752 – 1834) of Lyons. Although in use on the continent in 1801, his automatic pattern selector did not arrive in England unitl 1823. However, once installed, the Coventry weavers perfected the art of the jacquard ribbons so beautifully that they rivalled those from Lyons and St. Etienne. The jacquard loom was capable of the most complicated designs and was suitable also for the reproduction of black and white photographs and engravings. Many souvenir pictures were made and sold at exhibitions and important events.

The whimsical ways of fashion and world events have always influenced the ribbon industry and made it unstable. In 1860, with a sudden frivolous preference for feathers and velvet instead of the beautiful beribboned millinery which used up to ten metres to decorate each hat, the ribbon industry began to experience great hardship. Added to this, the price of silk rose because of the war in China and also the failure of the European and Indian silkworm crops.

When the industry collapsed in 1860, Thomas Stevens was determined to keep his workers in employment and used his experiments to produce pictures that would appeal to all tastes. By keeping his prices as low as possible, he managed to arouse enough interest and create enough demand to keep his workers busy. He started by selling his pictures on barrows in the market place. They soon became well known and were then framed and sold in shops. These are now collectors' pieces.

Many other manufacturers copied the idea of the Stevengraphs to see them out of the depression, but the name Thomas Stevens (1828 – 1888) has always been closely associated with this work.

No matter how far back one goes in the history of fashion, ribbon has played its part, but never more strongly than in the fashions of the nineteenth century. The Victorians were great embroiderers and used ribbon for embroidering dresses, blouses, coats, infants' pelisses, children's dresses and coats, as well as picture frames and fire screens.

There is very little authentic information as to the origin of the embroidery. It seems it was first introduced from China via the East India Company in 1860. In fact in Queen Anne's reign, silk was imported in large quantities and in its path appeared the dainty China ribbons.

The oldest exhibited specimens of ribbon embroidery worked in this country are said to be mid-eighteenth century. After enjoying long-term popularity, it waned for a while, to be revived at the beginning of the nineteenth century.

Ribbon quilts were also made; they were the English version of the Log Cabin patchwork quilts of North America and were made during the last quarter of the nineteenth century from ribbons used for hat trimmings (see colour plates 1 and 2).

Boot top bands were also very fashionable in Victorian times, when ladies wore high-legged button boots reaching to the knee. Inside the boot was a two to three inch satin band woven in a jacquard design. These were very expensive to produce, but formed the backbone of one Coventry business for many years.

It was not in fact until the sixteenth century that ribbons in the present form are seen and heard of, and only in the seventeenth century that they acquired the fascination which has lasted through to the imaginative uses of today's fashionable, easy-care ribbons.

In the following pages I aim to help you exploit the wealth of colour and variety of ribbon on the market now. All you need is a basic knowledge of sewing techniques, coupled with lots of enthusiasm and a certain amount of patience. So many looks and textures can be created with ribbon; it's easy to be original and develop your own individual style if you wish. On the other hand, if your aims are not so lofty, the book will provide you with lots of ideas and patterns which you can simply copy or adapt. I will illustrate some of the possibilities of using ribbon and appliqué, using simple techniques, all of which are explained with working diagrams. All the ideas in the book can be used with a good commercial pattern, using your own thoughts for colour and fabric. The section on weaving fabric is designed to inspire you to find a use for of all the fabrics you'd like to buy simply because you can't resist them.

I wish you some happy, fruitful hours weaving and sewing; creating some of your own 'Fashion with Ribbon'.

# 1. Basic Principles

## Tools and equipment for ribbon weaving

**1** You will need a firm flat padded surface measuring roughly 59cm x 44cm (23in x 17in). A cork board is ideal, it is light and easy to handle, and enables the pins to penetrate the cork, to anchor the weaving.

**2** Glass-headed pins; these are kinder to your fingers than the normal dressmaker's pins.

**3** Lightweight iron-on interfacing to bond ribbons together, making weaving easy to handle.

**4** A pair of sharp, medium-size scissors.

**5** Rouleau turner for pulling ribbons through weaving.

**6** Trimming and tapemaker, to make fabric trimming.

**7** Tape measure.

**8** Ribbon.

The rouleau turner, illustrated with the tools and equipment (see colour plate 3), is an extremely useful gadget for weaving ribbons quickly. To use it, simply weave the rouleau turner through the ribbons, place the ribbons on to the hook, close the latch pin, and pull the ribbon through the weaving. This method is far quicker and much easier than using your fingers.

## Estimating quantities

As ribbons can be quite expensive, it is a good idea to estimate the amount of ribbon you will use.

To do this, measure your pattern, i.e. yoke, cuff or cushion, and allow a 2.5cm (1in) seam allowance on all sides; cut the interfacing and pin it out on the board.

1  For the warp ribbons:
Divide the width of the interfacing by the width of the ribbon, and multiply by the length.

2  For the weft ribbons:
Divide the length of the interfacing by the width of the ribbons and multiply by the width; this will give you the amount of ribbon for the weft.

These two measurements added together give you the total amount of ribbon. The wider the ribbon, the less you will use; the narrower the ribbon, the more you will need.

## Choosing your ribbons for weaving

To help you choose the right kind of ribbons for weaving, or for any kind of fashion or furnishing project, there are a few guidelines you must follow.

*1*
*Estimating quantities.*

All the ribbons used for fashion and furnishing must be woven-edge ribbons; the cut-edge ribbons are for craft work only. The single-faced satin (shiny on one side only) ribbons are ideal for any ribbon weaving and appliqué work, as they are soft and pliable and lighter in weight than the double-faced (shiny on both sides), which are used mainly for tying bows for streamers where both sides of the ribbon will show.

The ideal choice for all fashion, furnishing and fashion accessories are the easy-care polyester satin and nylon velvets and the woven boil-proof jacquards and grosgrain ribbons. They will have a long and useful life, and can even be passed on as family heirlooms, so some thought and care ought to go into your choice of ribbons.

To create interesting textures, weave wide and narrow ribbons together to create a quilted look (see the turquoise three-piece suit on page 61) or try mixing the beautiful jacquard ribbons with velvets or satin. The polyester grosgrain ribbon is ideal for belts and purses, either woven together or used as an edging and top stitched in place as a decorative trim. Working with ribbons of one colour, but using different textures and widths, can have very attractive results. For an excitingly rich texture try weaving fabric with ribbon, either in the same

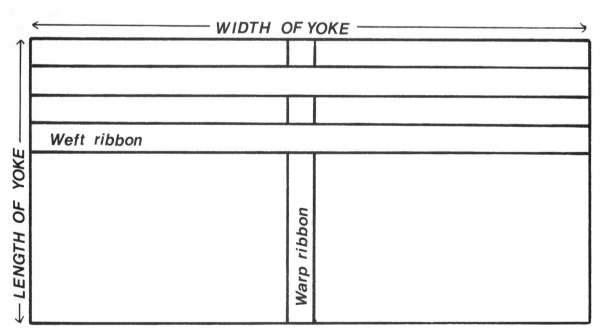

colours or using contrasts and in different widths.

It is also most important to use a good quality fabric for your garments or furnishing; do check that it will wash and wear well, or dry clean, as a lot of work goes into the weaving and appliqué and making up of garments. Plain fabrics with interesting textures are a good choice too, since ribbon work is often sufficient decoration in itself.

The garments in this book have been made up in an assortment of fabrics, i.e. wool, silk, cotton and some good quality mixtures of both natural and synthetic fibres. The table setting and the child's jacket are made from synthetic fibres because of the need to stand up to a good deal of laundering.

## Choosing your colour schemes

Choosing colour is a very personal thing and we all have very different ideas on the kind of colours we like to wear and to live with, and whether we like strong contrasts or colours that blend and tone harmoniously with each other. But one failsafe tip when choosing ribbons to weave for your garments or furnishings is to pick one ribbon to match as closely as possible the background fabric. This gives the weaving a look of being an integral part of the garment or furnishing.

Have your background fabric with you when choosing ribbons, as colour is very difficult to remember. Lay the ribbons on to the fabric and you will see immediately which looks good, and which to discard.

For cushions, the same principle applies; choose a ribbon to match your background fabric and again the weaving becomes part of the furnishing.

If you have a favourite colour that you love to wear, choose ribbons and fabric entirely in tones of this colour (monotone schemes) and the effect will be both elegant and sophisticated. Always check that the colours of the fabrics you buy suit you. To do this, simply drape the fabric around your neck and check with the mirror that you like what you see, just as you would with a bought garment. Many mistakes can be avoided by following this simple rule.

White fabric with white ribbon is both pretty and glamorous, and is a beautiful decoration for a christening gown or a wedding dress, and trimmed with white lace has a lovely luxurious effect. The combination of cream with beige is soft and warm and has an old world or antique flavour. Cream used with apricot, as in the table setting, becomes elegant without detracting from the relaxing and inviting atmosphere.

Rich, strong, dark colours, on the other hand, take a little more courage to wear, but can look really stunning. A red dress for instance trimmed with navy, or a purple blouse woven with fuschia pink, is most eye-catching. The important rule here is to balance the amount of contrast so that the two colours are not fighting for attention. Using one main colour for your garment and weaving a contrasting ribbon on yokes, cuffs and collar or belt would be a good balance. For a really cool, sophisticated look, black and white or navy and white are of course unbeatable.

A soft grey fabric with a matching ribbon combined with white is also a lovely look for a special occasion. The addition of ribbon to any of your garments or fashion accessories is an easy way of following the season's new fashion colours. Adding a new belt or bag made in a combination of colours that contrast or tone with your outfit brings it up-to-date instantly.

This is of course a guide; fashion itself is ever-changing and never static. Likewise you must be versatile, creating your own individual style.

# 2. Ribbon Weaving

## Plain weave

This is the simplest form of ribbon weaving and like other methods of weaving, consists of interlocking warp threads (vertical) with weft threads (horizontal), except that ribbon is used instead of yarns to create your own individual fabric. Many different patterns can be created by using various weaving sequences and a whole range of patterns and textures can be made by mixing various widths of ribbon, lace or broderie Anglaise.

The whole process is made very easy by weaving the ribbons over light-weight iron-on interfacing and with a warm iron, bonding the woven ribbons into fabric which is easy to handle. It is ideal for cutting out shapes and incorporating into either fashion garments or furnishing accessories.

The following example gives the measurements for a 38cm (15in) square, which could be used for a cushion, and allows for your seam allowance.

## Materials
6.6 metres (7¼yds) of 13mm (½in) single-faced satin ribbon in pale pink.
6.6 metres (7¼yds) of 13mm (½in) single-faced satin ribbon in darker pink.
6.6 metres (7¼yds) of 13mm (½in) single-faced satin ribbon in cream.
Glass-headed pins.
38cm (15in) square of lightweight iron-on interfacing.

## Method

### Warp ribbon
1 Pin the interfacing onto your cork board, adhesive side up.

2 Cut the ribbons into 38cm (15in) lengths and, starting at the top left hand corner, pin down the warp ribbons from top to bottom, laying them side by side, edges touching, and working in sequence – pale pink, darker pink, and cream until the interfacing is covered.

### Weft ribbon
1 Starting at the top right-hand corner, using a pale pink ribbon, weave under one, over one, under one, until the row is complete. Pin down firmly at both sides.

2 Weave the darker ribbon, over one, under one, over one, to the end of the row, pinning it down firmly.

3 Repeat the first row again, but this time with cream ribbon, weaving under one, over one, etc. until the row is complete.

Repeat this two-row pattern, using the three ribbons in sequence. Pale pink, darker pink, cream making sure the ribbons are close together, until interfacing is covered.

### Finishing
When the weaving is complete, dry press lightly over the ribbons as close to the pins as possible using a warm iron. Carefully remove the pins, and press the weaving again from the wrong side with a damp cloth, to bond the interfacing to the ribbons.

Trim the raw edges and machine 1cm (²⁄₅in) in from the edge. This eliminates any movement of ribbon around the edges, and your ribbon weaving is ready to be made up into a cushion or garment.

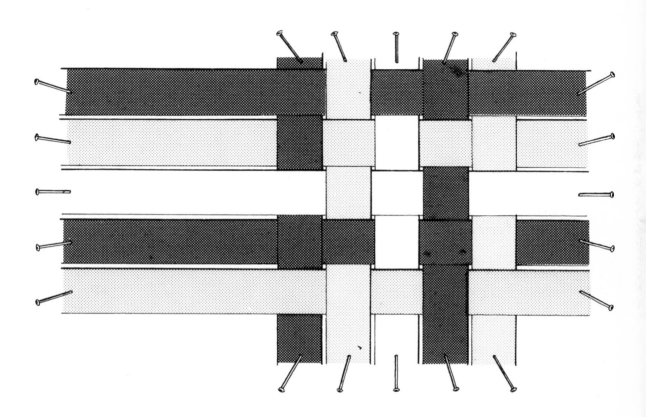

2
*Plain weave using three colours.*

## Bias weave

This is a most versatile weave and can look different each time you weave it, by simply using various widths of ribbon, or the way in which you weave together two different colours. Weaving one colour for the warp and another colour for the weft will give you a checker-board weave, but if you weave the two colours alternately across both warp and weft, you will weave the fabric into a stripe.

### Materials for a dress yoke
7 metres (7¾yds) of 13mm (½in) wide single satin pink ribbon.
7 metres (7¾yds) of 13mm (½in) wide single satin grey ribbon.
Lightweight interfacing.
Glass-headed pins.

### Method

*Warp ribbons (grey ribbon)*
**1** Fold interfacing on the diagonal to mark you bias centre, and mark with pencil.

**2** Place the first warp ribbon on this centre line, trim the ribbon and pin in place.

**3** Place the second warp ribbon on the right-hand side of the centre ribbon, and continue working on this side until the interfacing is covered, making sure all ribbons are close together. Continue to cut and pin down the warp ribbons on the left-hand side of the centre line, until the interfaceing is completely covered.

*Weft ribbon (pink ribbon)*
**1** Again starting in the bias centre with your second colour, weave the ribbon under one, over one, until the row is complete.

**2** Weave the second weft ribbon, over one, under one, to the end of the row, keeping it close to the first ribbon and working on the right-hand side of the centre until this part is complete. Weave the left-hand section in the same way until the weaving is completed.

To make a striped fabric, weave pink and grey alternately in both warp and weft. To keep ribbons taut and straight, place one or two pins in the centre; these can be moved along as the work progresses.

3
*Bias weave.*

## The quilted look (bias weave)

To create this luxurious look with your ribbons, you will need to use two different widths of ribbon in the same colour.

For the turquoise three-piece, I used 3mm and 10mm wide single-faced satin ribbon. To make up this design, cut your interfacing and estimate your quantities. Use the guide for the bias weave to find the bias centre and then proceed.

**1** Start from your bias centre and pin down the 10mm wide ribbon, then your 3mm wide ribbon close to it, now place your 10mm ribbon by the narrow one again and continue in this way until your interfacing is covered.

**2** To weave the weft ribbons, start again from the bias centre of your work and proceed as follows:

*4*
*Bias weave; quilted look using 10mm and 3mm ribbons.*

*Row one:* Take the 10mm ribbon and weave over the narrow ribbon and under the wide ribbon, to the end of the row.
*Row two:* Take the 3mm ribbon and weave over the wide ribbon, (10mm) and under the narrow ribbon, repeat to the end of the row.
*Row three:* The same as the first row. It is the narrow ribbons (3mm) being woven over the wider ribbons that produces the quilted look.

**3** Continue to weave from the centre to the right side of the yoke or cuff, and when this is complete, weave again from the centre to the left-hand side of your work. Sometimes it is easier to complete one half of the work, and then to turn the whole area around, so that you are in fact working at the same angle again.

**4** When all the weaving is complete, press gentle with a warm iron on the right side, then remove pins, turn the weaving to wrong side and press again with a damp cloth to make sure all the ribbons are in place.

**5** Cut our your yoke pattern and then machine all around the edge, about 1cm (2/5in) from the cut edge.

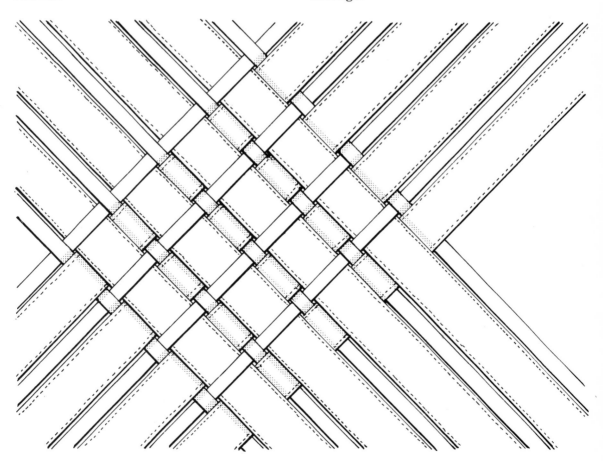

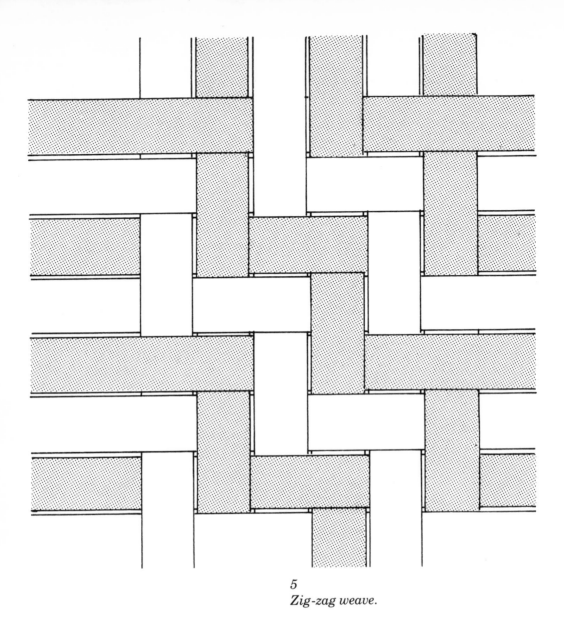

5
*Zig-zag weave.*

## *Zig-zag weave*

Two colours were used in this weave with ribbons of the same width, but different widths can be used and, when combined with ribbons of the same colour, make an interesting texture.

### Method

**1** Place the iron-on interfacing on your board adhesive side up.

**2** Pin down an odd number of warp ribbons. If two colours are used, begin and end with the same colour ribbon.

**To weave weft ribbons, alternate colour A and B as follows:**

*Row one:* Colour A, over two, under two, over two, to the end of the row.

*Row two:* Colour B under one, then over two, under two, over two. Repeat to the end.

*Row three:* Colour A under two, over two, under two, over two. Repeat to the end.

*Row four:* Colour B over one, then under two, over two, under two. Repeat to the end.

These four rows form the zig-zag pattern.

**4** Continue to weave rows 1-4 until the weaving is complete.

## Cube weave

This three-dimensional weave is woven in triple weaving, producing a cube pattern. It has the look of traditional patchwork.

Three ribbons are needed for this design, one dark ribbon and two lighter tones. Extra interest and depth was created for the cushion illustrated on page *105* by using rich velvet ribbons with a very beautiful jacquard ribbon.

**Materials** (to make a cushion 41cm (16in) square).
5 metres (5½yd) of 35mm (1½in) white nylon velvet ribbon.
5 metres (5½yd) of 35mm (1½in) green nylon velvet ribbon.
5 metres (5½yd) of 35mm (1½in) swiss-woven jacquard.
A piece of lightweight interfacing 44cm (17in) square.
50cm (½yd) of 90cm (36in) wide lining (backing).

Glass-headed pins.
20cm (8in) zip.

In this design, the warp consists of lengthwise strips of ribbon, and the weft of two sets of ribbons, one woven diagonally across the warp, from the top left-hand corner, and the other set from the right-hand corner.

This produces your patchwork pattern, and a material of three thicknesses. It is, therefore, very hard wearing and ideal for cushions.

### Method

*Warp ribbons* (white velvet ribbon)
**1** Pin the interfacing on a board, adhesive side up.
**2** Cut eleven lengths of white ribbon 44cm (17in) long, and pin them side by side until the interfacing is covered.

6
*Cube weave, first weft.*

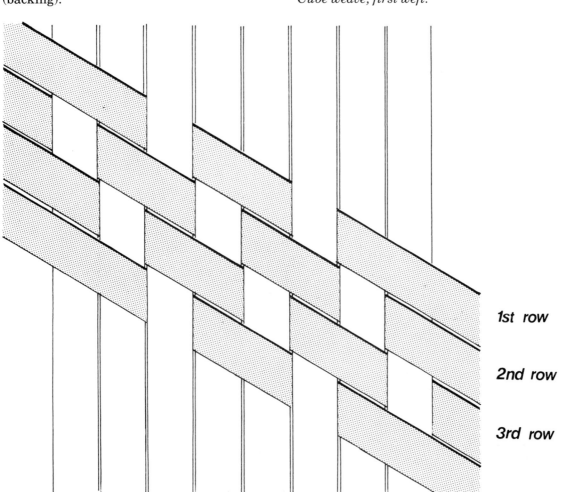

1st row

2nd row

3rd row

*First weft* (green velvet ribbon)

**3** Take the green velvet ribbon and weave diagonally from the top left-hand corner and place the first ribbon approximately one third of the way up from the bottom right-hand corner (14cm) (5½in).

*Row one:* over two, under one, repeat to end.

*Row two:* over one, *under one, over 2*, repeat from * to * to end of row.

*Row three:* under one, over two, repeat to end.

Repeat this three-row pattern to the bottom left-hand corner, cutting the ribbon and pinning down as you work. The cut ribbons can be used on the opposite side with no further cutting, avoiding waste.

**4** Now complete the weaving by working towards the top right-hand corner.

**7**
*Cube weave, second weft.*

*Second weft ribbon* (jacquard)

**5** When working the second weft ribbon, a few of the pins already placed around the edge will need to be removed and repinned as you weave. Beginning at the top right-hand corner, weave diagonally across towards the left in the following three-row pattern, placing the first ribbon one-third of the way up from the bottom left-hand corner (14cm) (5½in).

*Row one:* over one, under two, repeat to end of row.

*Row two:* under one, * over one, under two, * repeat to end. From * to *.

*Row three:* Under two, over one, repeat to end of row.

Repeat these three rows, working towards the bottom right-hand corner. Complete the weaving by working towards the top left-hand corner.

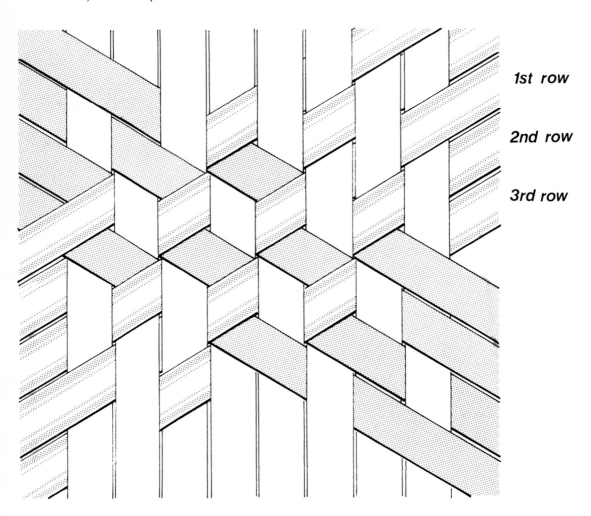

**1st row**

**2nd row**

**3rd row**

**6** This pattern refers to weaving over and under the upright warp ribbon. The second weft, however, also passes under and over the first weft ribbon, and can only be achieved if the angle is correct.

Weaving this double weft in three colours, one dark and two lighter shades, makes an interesting cube design and is well worth the effort involved.

**7** When all weaving is complete, carefully remove the pins and tack round the edges to hold all the ribbons in place. Trim the weaving to shape and press carefully on the back with a damp cloth and steam iron.

## Weaving with fabric

This is a very economical way of using up your odd fabric pieces and makes a very decorative finish for any fashion garment, table decoration or furnishing accessory. Any weave can be worked with fabric, just as it can with ribbon. Weaving with matching or contrasting ribbon, or using two different widths of fabrics, depending on the texture and look you wish to create, make the possibilities endless. Half a metre of fabric will give you lots of trim to weave areas such as yokes, cuffs and pockets, or cushion covers and table mats.

**Materials** (for the trim)
50cm (½yd) of 90cm (36in) wide fabric.
Trimming and tape maker 25mm and 12mm.
5 metres (5½yd) of 10mm-wide single satin ribbon.
Lightweight iron-on interfacing.

Any light or medium-weight fabric can be used with the tape maker.

**Method**
**1** Cut the fabric on the bias into strips measuring 48mm (1⅞in) or 25mm (1in) wide. If your fabric is very fine, you may need to cut it slightly wider.

**2** Feed the fabric through the wide end of the tape maker and press the folded trim as it is pulled through. Continue to press all the pieces until you have enough trim to start weaving.

*8*
*Making the fabric trim for weaving.*

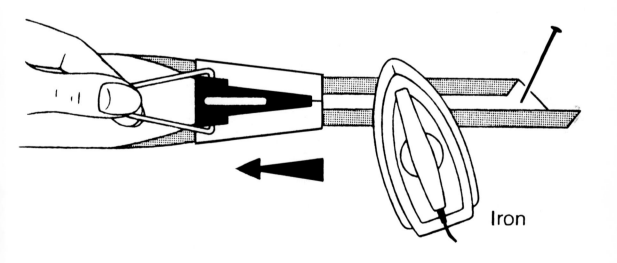

Iron

## Striped weave

**1** Cut your interfacing with a 2.5cm (1in) seam allowance all round and pin adhesive side up on your cork board.

**2** Start from the bias centre and pin one length of fabric, one ribbon, one fabric; repeat until the interfacing is covered (*figure 9*).

*9*
*Fabric and ribbon pinned out on the bias grain.*

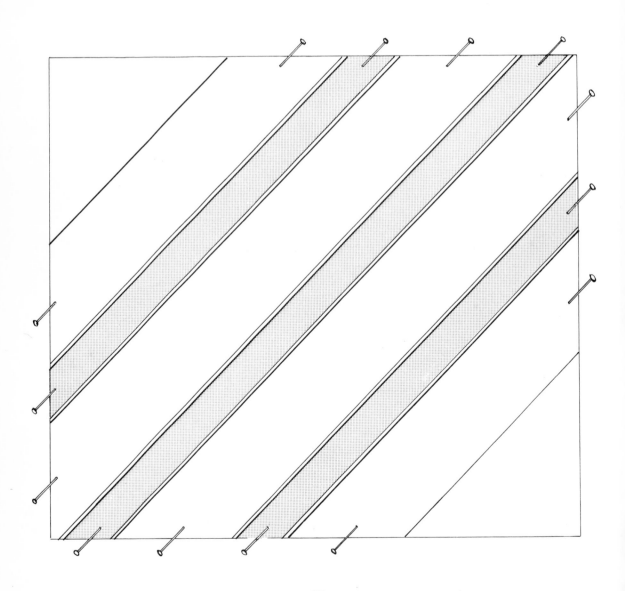

**3** Weave weft ribbons again from the bias centre (*figure 10*). To make it appear striped, weave the fabric trim under the fabric and over the ribbon; weave the ribbon under the ribbon and over the fabric.

**4** Repeat until the weaving is complete, pinning ribbons and fabric to board and trimming as you work.

Because the fabric is cut on the bias grain, it is very easy to handle and weave.

This same design, or any other weaving design, can be used for weaving with fabrics alone; in the same widths or by using two different widths and colours, depending on the colour schemes and textures you wish to create.

*10*
*Fabric and ribbon woven on the bias grain.*

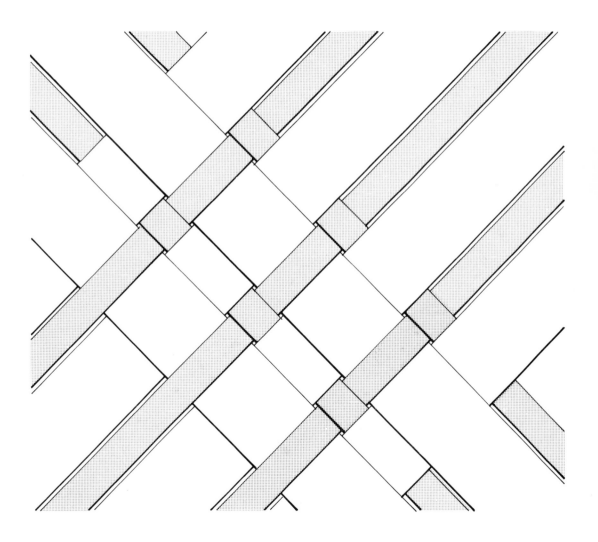

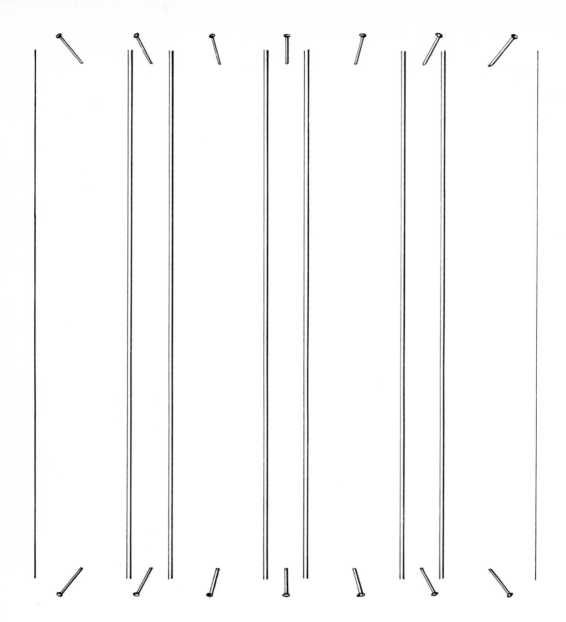

**11**
*Fabric and ribbon pinned out on the straight grain.*

*1. Bed quilt made from pure silk Coventry ribbons made by Mrs. Martha Walker for her granddaughter's marriage, 1895. The centre is made from silk ribbon pieces with borders of printed cottons.*

*2. Centre piece donated to the Herbert Art Gallery, Coventry, by Mr. and Mrs. J. T. Stringer of Coventry. Made from weavers' ends of pure silk ribbon.*

3. Tools and equipment.

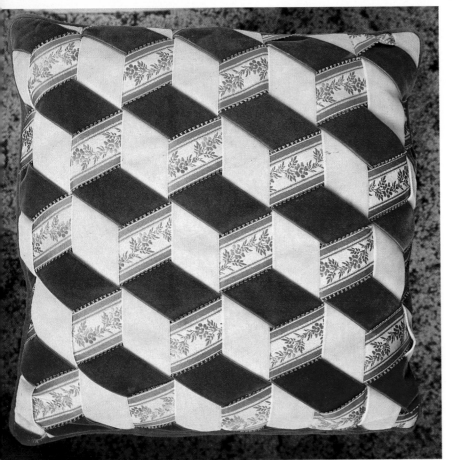

4. A cube weave cushion,
woven in two shades of
velvet ribbon and one
jacquard ribbon.

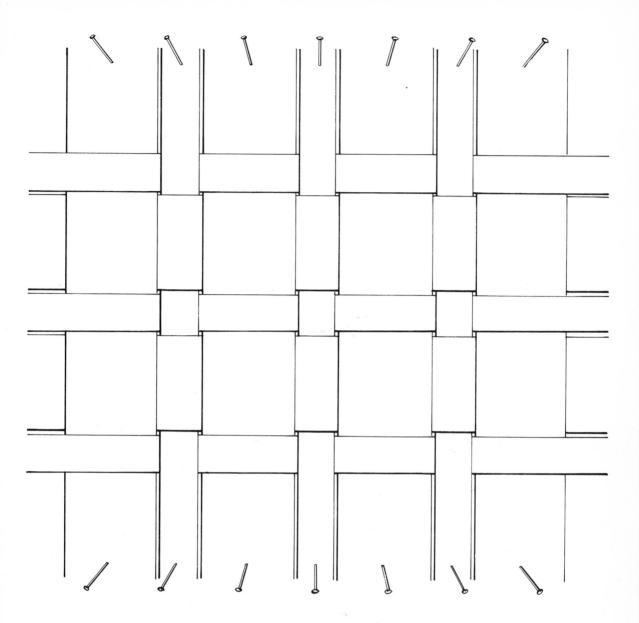

*12*
*Fabric and ribbon woven on the straight grain.*

Fabric can also be used on the straight grain when it is even more economical to use. The table set (colour plate 20) was made with economy in mind. Figures 11 and 12 illustrate one method of weaving fabric alone, in a plain weave.

Using the fabric on the straight grain is also ideal for school projects, not only for easy cutting and economy, but because younger students are inclined to reduce bias strips to lengths of string. For fashion garments, however, the bias grain has more ease of movement and will therefore hang and fit better with no fraying edges.

Weaving fabric with ribbon is a wonderful way of building up areas of interest and texture. Both the gold shirt dress and the white blouse have panels of fabric and ribbon, woven in the bias weave, with a 13mm wide ribbon.

Both front and back panels of the dress are stitched into the raglan sleeve seams. The fabric was cut on the bias grain and used 2 metres (2yd) of 150cm (60in) wide fabric and a total of 23 metres (25yd) of black satin ribbon. Creating the same effect on the blouse required an extra half metre (20in) of fabric and 12 metres (13yd) of satin ribbon.

The purple and pink blouse relies on fabric alone for the decorative yoke and collar sections and required an extra 30cm (12in) of both the colours. The fabric was cut and woven on the bias grain into a striped design.

Weaving the epaulets for the travel coat was less time consuming, as the wider trimming was used with the 13mm ribbon, creating the same effect as the blue and grey outfit (*fig. 68*).

The illustration of the wedding gown (*figure 75*) depicts a large, shaped area of the front and back bodice woven with fabric and ribbon and embellished with small pearls and rhinestones. To create this look successfully, a lightweight fabric, such as silk taffeta, would need to be used to eliminate the risk of any additional bulk in darts or side seams. The collar and cuffs are made in the same design.

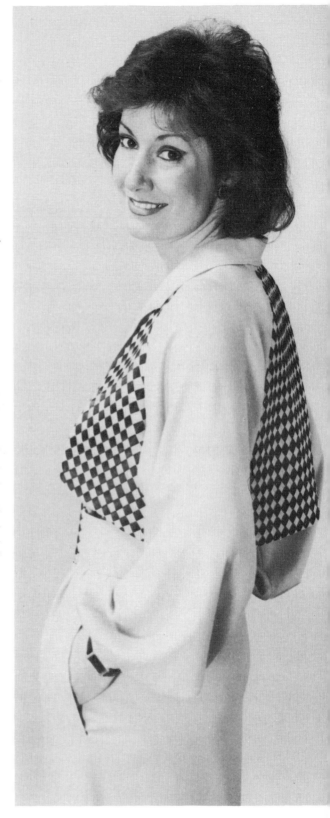

*13*
*Gold shirt dress; ribbon and fabric woven panels in black and gold.*

*14*
*Fabric and ribbon woven with 4x3mm-wide*
*ribbons and fabric 12mm wide.*

*15*
*White cotton blouse.*

28

*16*
*Close-up of pocket of white blouse.*

*Purple and pink blouse showing fabric weaving.*

# 3. Projects

## A baby's christening robe and bonnet

This beautiful christening robe (*colour plate 5*), with its ribbon-woven yoke and lace trim, is cut on classically simple lines. The tucked and frilled skirt is open down the centre back and gathered into the lined yoke. The short puffed sleeves are gathered into a narrow band and trimmed with lace. Ribbons of two different widths woven in plain weave and trimmed with lace were also used to decorate the shaped and lined bonnet. The lower edge of the bonnet is encased with a wide bias band, the ribbon being threaded through to tie under the chin.

The robe will fit a baby up to nine months old and could be made in either polyester silk or satin, or fine white lawn.

### Christening robe materials
2 metres (2¼yd) of 115cm (45in) wide white polyester silk.
4 metres 50cm (5yd) of 5cm (2in) wide lace.
4 metres 50cm (5yd) of 6mm wide polyester single-faced satin ribbon.
4 metres 50 cem (5yd) of 3mm wide polyester single-faced satin ribbon.
Sewing thread and silk pins.
Paper for pattern and pencil.
Lightweight iron-on interfacing.
Two 7mm nylon snap fasteners.

### To weave the front yoke in plain weave
**1** Cut out one piece of interfacing measuring 26cm x 13cm (10in x 5in) and place it adhesive side up on your board.

**2** Pin out the warp ribbons as described on page 14, starting with your centre front line and using the 6mm ribbon.

**3** Pin the ribbons in sequence, i.e. one 6mm ribbon and then one 3mm ribbon, laying them side by side, working from centre to left, and from centre to right, until the interfacing is covered. (It is better when working a relatively small area like this to start in the centre, as it helps to keep your weaving straight and accurate.)

**4** To weave the weft ribbons, start again with the 6mm ribbon, and this time weave the first ribbon just inside your seam allowance along the lower edge (this gives a very good sewing guide) and weave in the simple plain weave keeping the ribbons in sequence, i.e. one 3mm and one 6mm ribbon, until the weaving is complete.

**5** Finish by pressing gently on the right side, remove the pins, press on the reverse side with a damp cloth.

### Pattern
Enlarge the pattern pieces [each square represents 1cm (³⁄₈in)] and add on a seam allowance of 1½cm (⁵⁄₈in) on all pieces except the neckline, which has a bias-bound edge.

*Cutting out*
Place front yoke pattern on the ribbon weaving and cut out one front yoke section. Machine 1cm (³⁄₈in) in from the edge all round to hold ribbons in place. Fold fabric selvedge edges together and cut out all pattern pieces. Cut frill sections by cutting two pieces measuring 56cm x 12cm (22in x 4¾in) (back sections) and one piece measuring 115cm x 12cm (45in x 4¾in) (front section). The front skirt is cut to a folded edge, the back skirt to the selvedge edge.

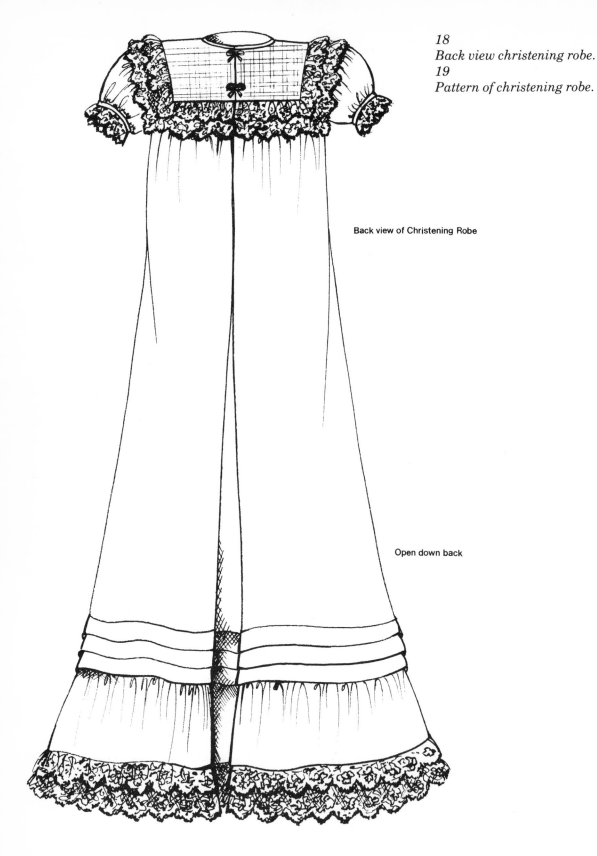

**Back view of Christening Robe**

Open down back

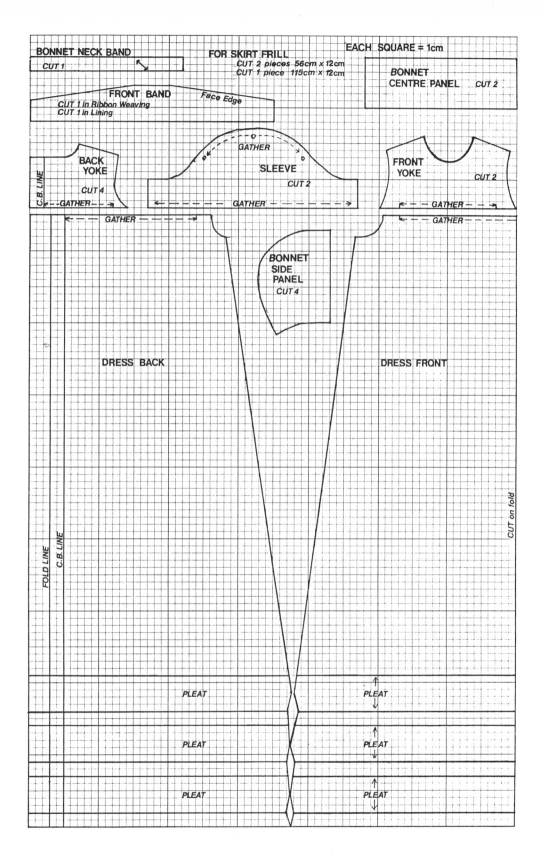

BONNET NECK BAND

CUT 1

FOR SKIRT FRILL
CUT 2 pieces 56cm x 12cm
CUT 1 piece 115cm x 12cm

EACH SQUARE = 1cm

BONNET
CENTRE PANEL    CUT 2

FRONT BAND    Face Edge

CUT 1 in Ribbon Weaving
CUT 1 in Lining

BACK
YOKE

CUT 4

C.B. LINE

GATHER

GATHER

SLEEVE

CUT 2

GATHER

FRONT
YOKE

CUT 2

GATHER

GATHER

GATHER

BONNET
SIDE
PANEL
CUT 4

DRESS BACK

DRESS FRONT

FOLD LINE

C.B. LINE

CUT on fold

PLEAT

PLEAT

PLEAT

PLEAT

PLEAT

PLEAT

33

## Making up: order of work

### Yoke

**1** Stitch the back yoke sections and front yoke sections (ribbon yoke) at the shoulder with a flat seam. Trim and press open. Pin the bound edge of the lace trim on to the yoke over seam lines as shown. Turn in 13mm (½in) of the lace ends at centre back (*fig. 1*).

### Skirt

**2** Stitch front and back skirts together at the side seams with a French seam, leaving skirts open down the centre back. Gather the top edge of the skirt with two rows of large machine stitches.

### Frill

To make up the frill, machine together with a french seam, placing one back section either side of the front section and leaving open at the centre back. These seams will eventually align with the side seam on the skirt (*fig. 2*)

**3** Gather the top edge of the frill with two rows of machine stitches (*fig. 2*).

**4** Pin and bound edges of lace over the hem seam lines and tack in place; fold the hem over the lace to encase the lace in the hem and machine in place (*fig. 3*).

**5** Pin the frill to the lower edge of the skirt and adjust the gathers, align seams in frill with side seams in skirt and machine in place. Trim the frill seam and encase raw edges in the skirt seam; press upwards.

**6** Make 2½cm (1in) tucks on the outside of the skirt and press downwards. (The lower tuck covers the frill seam.) (*fig. 4*).

**7** Make a 6mm (¼in) single seam along the back of the skirt and frill. Machine in place. Fold the self facing along the fold line. Tack in place and press.

**8** Pin front and back yoke to the upper edges of the skirt and adjust gathers; tack and machine

in place. Trim and press and the seam upwards (*fig. 5*).

**9** Make up the yoke facing. Pin the yoke facing to the back yoke along centre back line and machine in place (*fig. 6*). Trim the seam and turn the facing to the inside to line the yoke. Tack in place around the neck and armholes.

**10** To finish the neckline with a bias strip, cut out a piece of fabric 2.5cm x 31cm (1in x 12in). With right sides together and edges even, pin the binding to neck edge extending ends 13mm (½in) beyond the back edges. Stitch and press the seam up. Trim the seam. Turn in the ends and press. Fold over the raw edge and slip to the neck seam.

### Sleeves

**11** Gather the lower edges of the sleeves between the seam lines and the upper edges between the balance points.

**12** Pin the lace to the sleeve bands, just inside the seam allowance and having a 13mm (½in) seam on both ends of the lace. Place the facing on top of the lace and machine along the seam line, through the three layers (*fig. 7*). Trim, turn and press.

**13** Gather the sleeve onto the band, adjusting gathers. Pin, tack and machine in place. Trim and press the seam downwards.

**14** Stitch the sleeve seam together with the French seam. Press to one side. Hand-stitch the sleeve facing band to the inside of the sleeve.

**15** Pin the sleeves into the armholes, adjusting gathers; tack and machine. Stitch again 3mm (⅛in) away. Trim and seam. Press the seam with great care towards the sleeve. Neaten seam by oversewing to eliminate fraying.

### To finish the back neck

**16** Sew two 7mm nylon snap fasteners to the back yoke at the neck edge.

**17** Make two small bows with the 3mm ribbon and stitch securely in place. Each bow uses 18cm (7in) of ribbon (*fig. 8*).

20
*Working drawings of christening robe (figures 1-12).*

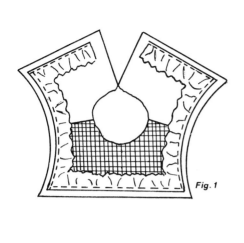

Fig. 1

Frill

Fig 2

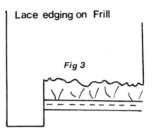

Lace edging on Frill

Fig 3

c
B

Tucks in Skirt

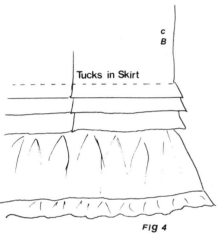

Fig 4

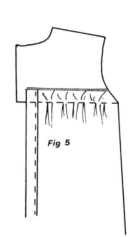

Fig 5

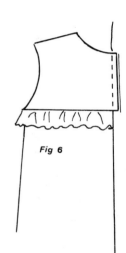

Fig 6

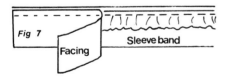

Fig 7

Facing

Sleeve band

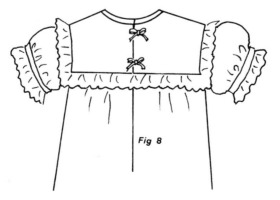

Fig 8

# Christening bonnet

## Materials
6 metres (6½yd) of 6mm-wide single-faced satin ribbon.
6 metres (6½yd) of 3mm-wide single-faced satin ribbon.
70cm (¾yd) of 13mm-wide double-faced satin ribbon for the neck edge.
80cm (1yd) of gathered lace trim.

It takes roughly one hour to weave the ribbon trim band for the bonnet, and about two hours to complete the making up.

## To weave the band
1 Cut out the interfacing with a seam allowance and lay adhesive side up on your board.

2 Lay out the warp ribbons (*fig. 9*) starting with a 6mm-wide ribbon, and pin it on to the straight edge inside your seam allowance. By doing this you have a guideline for your stitching later on. Continue to pin out warp ribbons, laying one 6mm ribbon and one 3mm ribbon side by side, until the interfacing is covered.

3 To weave the weft ribbons, start in the centre of the band with a 6mm-wide ribbon, then continue to weave in plain weave using alternate widths (i.e. one 3mm, one 6mm) from the centre to bottom and from centre to top. By weaving from centre up and then down, the weaving is kept very accurate and is quickly finished.

## To make the bonnet
1 Pin, tack and machine the bound edge of the lace over seam lines on all sides of the ribbon weaving band (*fig. 10*).

2 Pin the lining and stitch along the straight edge. Trim the seam, turn, press and tack the raw edges together (*fig. 11*).

3 Pin, tack and machine the side pieces of the bonnet to the centre section. Trim the seam and press it towards the centre. Make up the lining in the same way.

4 Pin and tack the wrong side of the band to the right side of the bonnet. Tack the right side of the lining to the right side of the band and machine this front edge. Trim the seam and turn, so the lining is now inside the bonnet.

5 Cut a bias strip 25cm x 4cm (10in x 1½in).

6 Fold in a 13mm (½in) seam at both ends of the bias strip and, keeping edges together, sew the strip to the neck edge. Trim the seam, fold over the raw edge and slip stitch to the seam, leaving the ends open.

7 Using a rouleau turner or a bodkin, thread the 13mm ribbon through the neckline and gather it to fit (*fig. 12*).

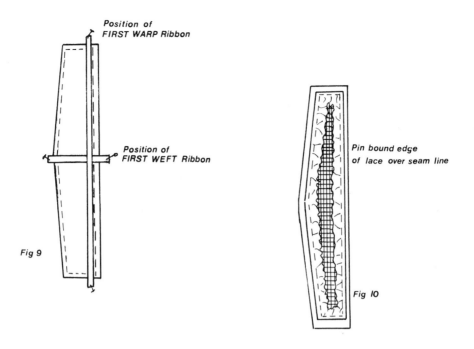

Position of
FIRST WARP Ribbon

Position of
FIRST WEFT Ribbon

Fig 9

Pin bound edge
of lace over seam line

Fig 10

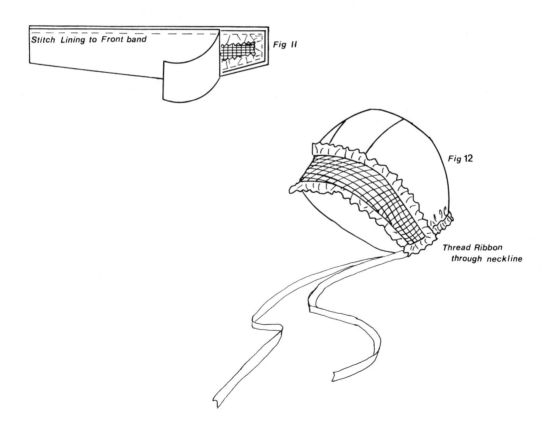

Stitch Lining to Front band

Fig II

Fig 12

Thread Ribbon
through neckline

# Baby's decorative bib

This baby's bib is made up in a cotton lawn using a simple pattern. It illustrates how ribbons can be used decoratively by simply top stitching in place with a small zig-zag stitch or stitching along either side of the width of the ribbon. This same technique was used to decorate the dressing gown on page 76. The bib is very economical to make. A 20cm (¼yd) length of cotton lawn 90cm (36in) wide will make three bibs, cutting them side by side across the width of the fabric. A total of 3 metres 20cm (3½yd) of ribbon in various colours and widths was used, and once you have selected your ribbons, it is wonderfully simple to sew and would make an ideal gift for a small baby.

## Materials

20cm (¼yd) of 90cm (36in) wide white cotton lawn.
60cm (¾yd) of 10mm single-faced satin ribbon in white.
60cm (¾yd) of 5mm picot-edge satin ribbon in cream.
1 metre 80 cm (1yd 31in) of 5mm picot-edge satin ribbon in pink.
Sewing thread to match your ribbons.
Dressmaker graph paper and pencil, and pins.

## Pattern

Enlarge pattern [*two* squares = 1cm (⅜in)]. This pattern is half scale and includes a 1cm (⅜in) seam allowance. Cut out the pattern in the cotton lawn. Cut a 2.5cm (1in) wide strip of bias fabric 20cm (8in) long.

21
*Baby's bib.*

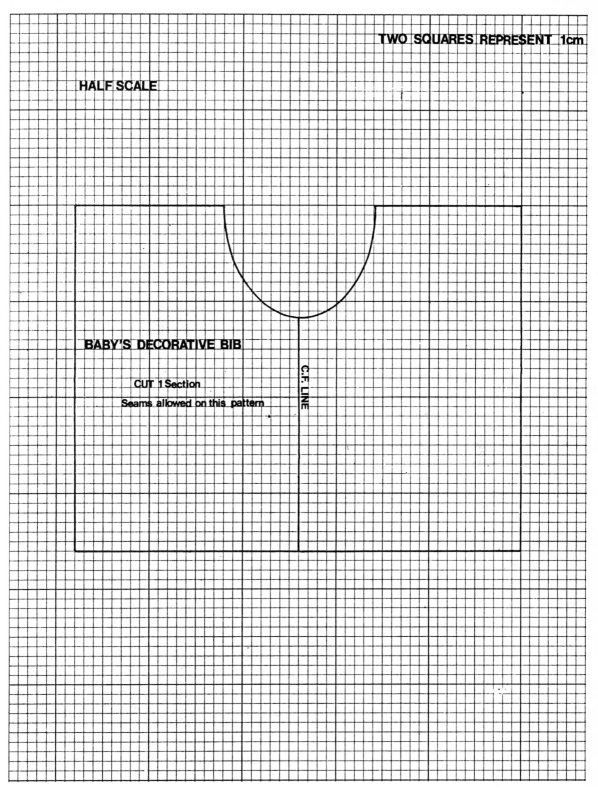

TWO SQUARES REPRESENT 1cm

HALF SCALE

BABY'S DECORATIVE BIB

CUT 1 Section

Seams allowed on this pattern

C.F. LINE

22
Pattern for baby's bib.

## To make up the bib

**1** Bind the neck edge with the bias strip. With right sides together, and edges even, pin the binding to the neck edge, extending 6mm (¼in) beyond the back edges (*fig. 1*). Stitch and press the seam up. Turn in the ends and press. Fold over the raw edge and slip stitch to the seam (*fig. 2*).

**2** Pin and tack a 1cm (⅜in) seam on all edges on to the right side of the bib (*fig. 3*). Press.

**3** Following the diagram in figure 4, machine the white ribbons in position with a straight stitch along either edge of the ribbon, so that the ribbon now covers the raw seam completely.

**4** Place the cream picot edge ribbon 1cm (⅜in) in from the white ribbon, and following the same sequence, machine in place with a small zig-zag stitch down the centre of the ribbon. Machine the pink ribbon in position in the same way.

**5** Pin the bound edge of the lace trim over the raw seam at the shoulder and outside the white satin ribbon. Machine in place.

**6** Leaving an extension of 25cm (10in), place the remaining pink ribbon over the bound edge of the lace and machine in place with a small zig-zag stitch (*fig. 5*).

*23*
*Working drawings of baby's bib (figures 1-5).*

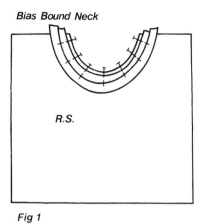

Bias Bound Neck

R.S.

Fig 1

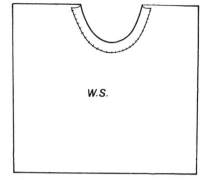

W.S.

Fig 2

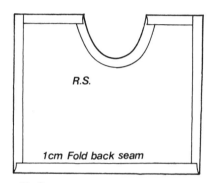

R.S.

1cm Fold back seam

Fig 3

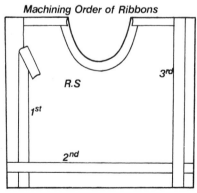

Machining Order of Ribbons

R.S

1st

2nd

3rd

Fig 4

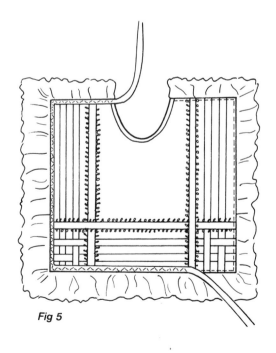

Fig 5

# Small child's detachable collar

This attractive child's collar, with its lace trimming and woven in brightly coloured ribbons, has a lovely shot appearance and adds a rich texture to any child's dress. The ribbons are woven in plain weave, and because of its size, this makes a very simple and easy project for a beginner to make. It has a single button fastening with ribbon at the centre back and looks equally pretty without the lace trimming. Optional ribbon ties can be attached at the sides. Contrasting colours were used in red, green and cream for a bright, cheerful look.

*24*
*Child's detachable collar.*

## Materials

20cm (8in) lining fabric (polycotton was used for this collar).
10 metres (11yd) of 7mm wide (¼in) cream single-faced satin ribbon.
7 metres (7¾yd) of 7mm wide (¼in) red single-faced satin ribbon.
2 metres (2¼yd) of 3mm wide (⅛in) green double-faced satin ribbon.
90cm (1yd) of 4cm wide 1½in) gathered lace.
Lightweight iron-on interfacing.
1 small pearl button.
Matching sewing thread.
Glass headed pins.
Paper for pattern, and pencil.

This collar is made to fit a size 18 months (86) but is suitable for any age group.

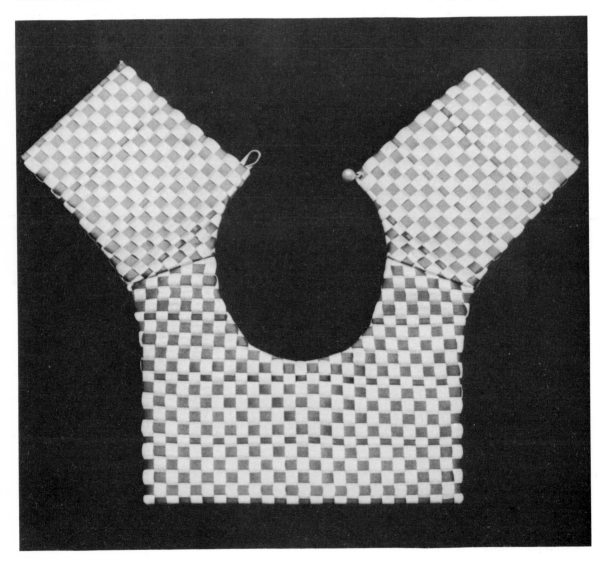

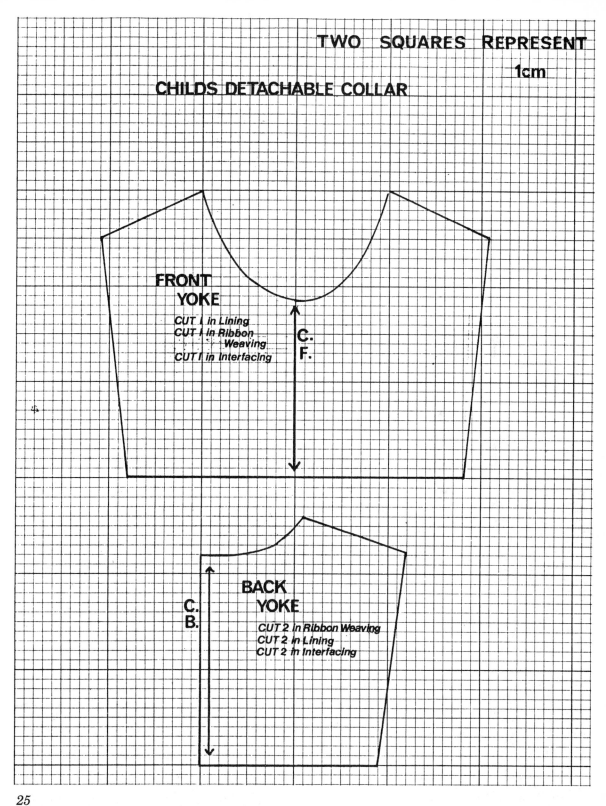

CHILDS DETACHABLE COLLAR

**FRONT
YOKE**

CUT 1 in Lining
CUT 1 in Ribbon
Weaving
CUT 1 in Interfacing

C.
F.

C.
B.

**BACK
YOKE**

CUT 2 in Ribbon Weaving
CUT 2 in Lining
CUT 2 in Interfacing

25
*Pattern for child's detachable collar.*

## Pattern (half scale)

**1** Enlarge pattern pieces [*two* squares represent 1cm (3/8in)] and add on a seam allowance of 1½cm (5/8in) on all pieces.

**2** Cut yoke sections out in the iron-on interfacing. Do not cut around the neck shape, simply cut straight across from the shoulder. This is to make the weaving easier. The shape is then recut when the weaving is completed.

**3** Pin the yoke shapes onto your board, adhesive side up, and side by side, so that the three sections are in a row. Position both back yoke sections together edge to edge along centre back, to enable you to weave these two sections as one piece. Separate when weaving is completed by cutting down the centre back line. Working these two sections together is both time saving and accurate and less wasteful with ribbons.

## Weaving the collar

To achieve the lovely shot effect on this collar, looking red from one angle and cream from another, the ribbons are woven using cream for the warp and red and green for the weft.

### Pinning out the warp ribbons

To achieve this effect, start by pinning out the cream ribbons along the length of the yoke, and by placing the first ribbon down the centre front line, work to the left and right of this line until the yoke section is covered. Pin the cream ribbons over the back yokes in the same way, starting at the centre back, and again working to the left and right of this line until both these yoke sections are covered with the cream ribbon.

### To weave your weft ribbons

**1** Starting with your 3mm green ribbon and weaving in plain weave, place this ribbon outside your seam allowance along the lower edge (this can be used later as your sewing guide for a straight line, with the green ribbon showing at the lower edge) (*fig. 1*).

**2** *Weave four rows in the 7mm red ribbon.

**3** Weave one row in the 3mm green ribbon.*

**4** Repeat these two rows of pattern in plain weave until the yokes are completed.

Finish the weaving by adding one row of red ribbon below the first green ribbon; this row will be inside your seam allowance. Finish by pressing gently on the right side. Remove pins and press on the reverse side with a damp cloth. Separate the back yokes by cutting along the centre back line. Place the pattern on top of the woven yokes, pin in position and recut neck edges and trim all around edges. Remove patterns. Machine all around each yoke section just inside the seam allowance to hold the ribbons in place. Press again.

## To make up collar

**1** Cut out the lining. Pin, tack and machine shoulder seams together on lining and woven yokes with a flat seam. Press seams open and trim to 1cm (½in).

**2** Pin bound edge of lace trim onto the woven yokes across the lower edges at the back and over the shoulders and across the front. Tack in position (*fig. 2*).

**3** Place the collar lining right sides together over the woven yokes. Pin and tack the layers together around neck edge, outer edges and down one side of the centre back edge, leaving 6cm (2¼in) gap open in one back edge for turning the collar through. Machine in position (*fig. 3*). Trim seam allowance, notch the curves and trim corners diagonally.

**4** Turn the collar to the right side, tack and carefully press all seamed edges.

**5** Slip stitch the gap in the centre back.

**6** Make a small button loop at the back neck with a 5cm (2in) length of ribbon and stitch in place by hand.

**7** Sew a small pearl button on the opposite side.

## Optional ribbon ties

**8** Use 1 metre 10cm (1¼yd) of 10mm wide double-faced satin ribbon. Cut the ribbon into four equal pieces. Position ribbon ties 1cm (½in) above the lower front and back edges of the collar and hand-sew in place. Cut the loose edges of the ribbon into a fish-tail to prevent the ends from fraying (*fig. 4*).

*26*
*Working drawings for child's detachable collar (figures 1-4).*

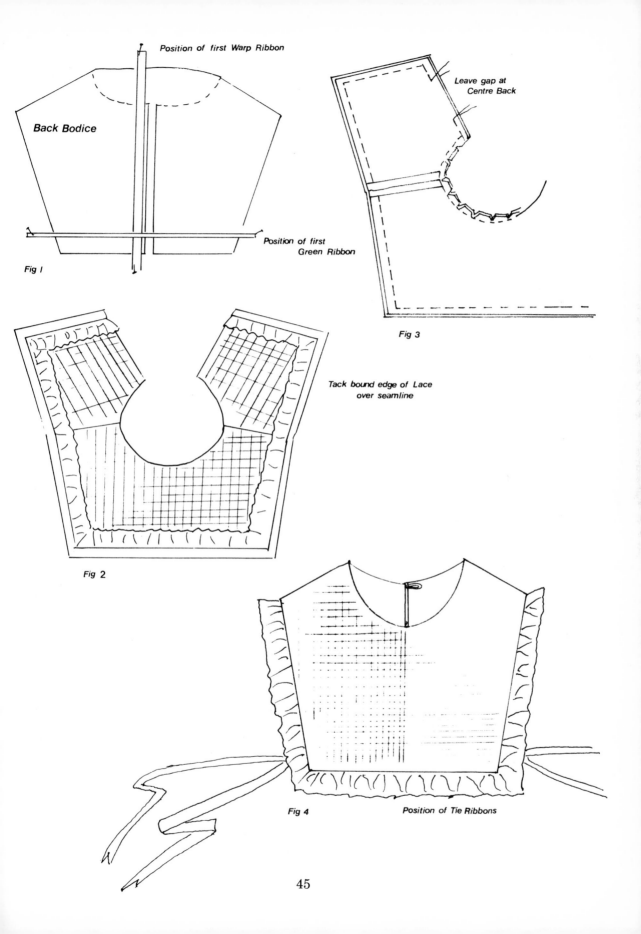

Position of first Warp Ribbon

Back Bodice

Position of first
Green Ribbon

Fig 1

Leave gap at
Centre Back

Fig 3

Tack bound edge of Lace
over seamline

Fig 2

Fig 4

Position of Tie Ribbons

28
*Child's quilted jacket showing the detachable
sleeve.*

46

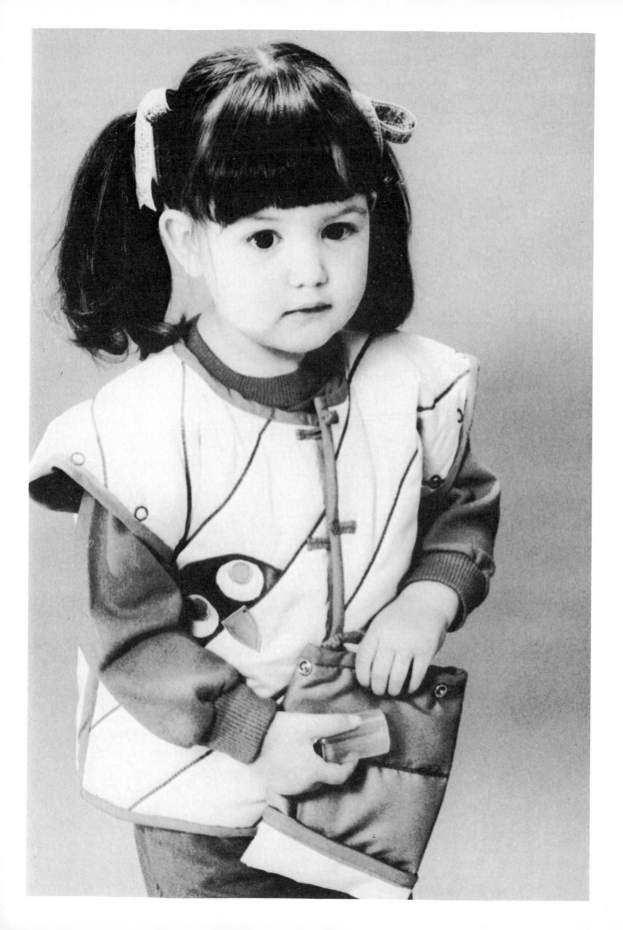

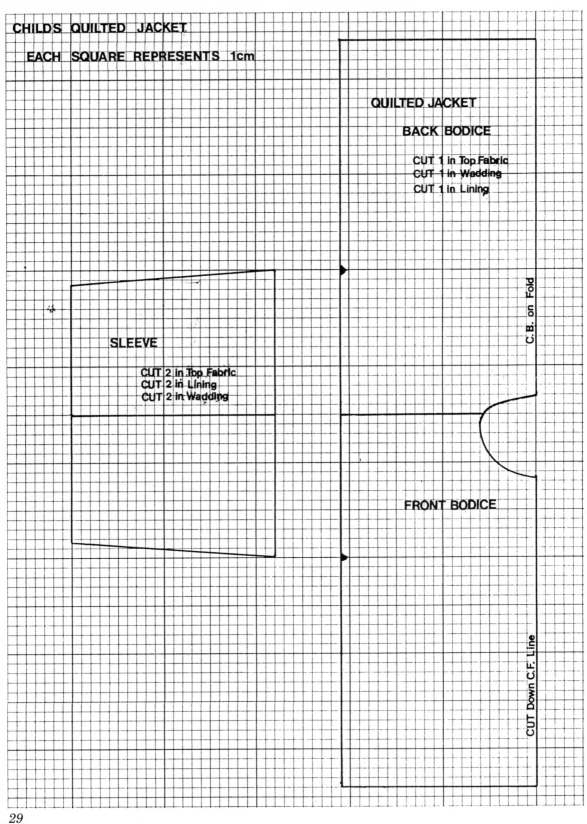

CHILD'S QUILTED JACKET

EACH SQUARE REPRESENTS 1cm

QUILTED JACKET

BACK BODICE

CUT 1 in Top Fabric
CUT 1 in Wadding
CUT 1 in Lining

C.B. on Fold

SLEEVE

CUT 2 in Top Fabric
CUT 2 in Lining
CUT 2 in Wadding

FRONT BODICE

CUT Down C.F. Line

29
*Pattern of child's quilted jacket.*

5. *Christening robe and bonnet.*

6. *The collar, cuffs and shoulder line of this evening gown have ribbons of a matching shade woven together in the bias weave.*

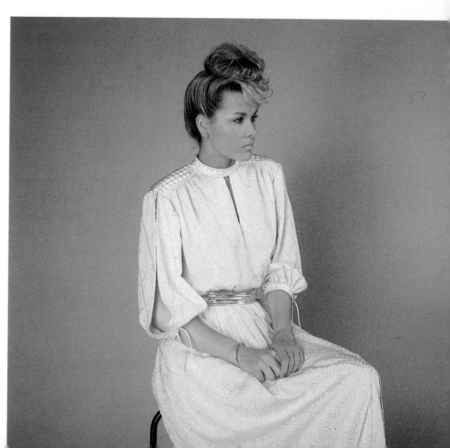

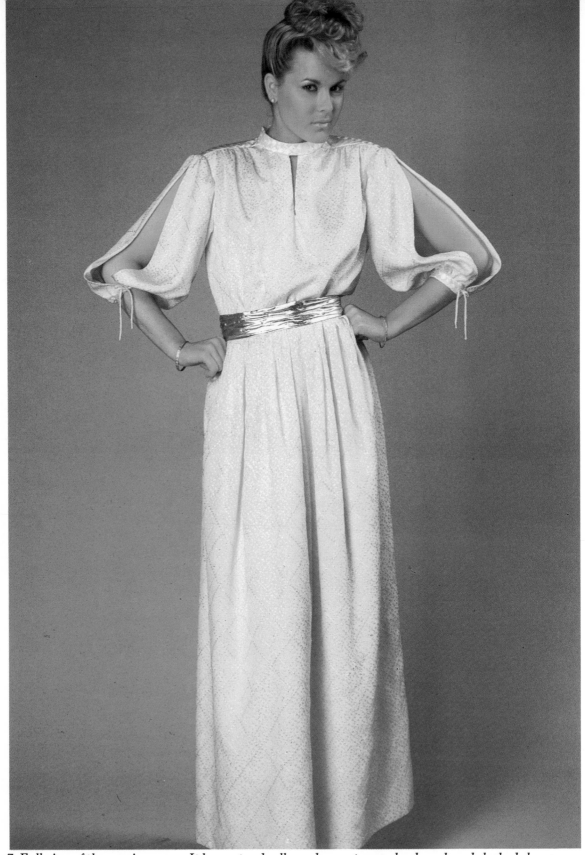

*7. Full view of the evening gown. It has a stand collar, a deep cut-away back neck and slashed sleeves.*

8. *Turquoise three-piece suit using two widths of ribbon to give the appearance of quilting.*

9. *Polyester silk blouse using the wide ribbon for appliqué and for covering the buttons on the front fastening. The narrow ribbon, using the shuttle technique, was used to decorate both sleeves, collar and bodice of blouse.*

10. Dusky pink and silver-grey ribbons were woven into the checker-board design with the bias weave for the yoke of this grey two-piece suit.

11. Sleeveless velvet jacket using the narrow ribbon for embroidery and wide ribbon for appliqué.

## Child's quilted jacket with detachable sleeves

It is always very satisfying to make something practical and pretty for a small child. This colourful quilted jacket, cut in a rectangle with detachable sleeves, is practical, eye-catching and quick to make. All the edges are bound with a bias trimming. The bird appliqué is based on a simple half-circle and small-circle design. Children always look good in strong bright colours, so this jacket was made with bright yellow polyester cotton lined with the same quality fabric in turquoise and quilted and bound with red ribbon. The sleeves are worn with the turquoise side showing and the yellow used as the lining, shown in the turn-back cuff. This pattern will fit children from 2½ years to 4 years old, but you will need to check the length of the jacket and the sleeve length. The children in the picture are 2½ years and 4 years old. A 2oz. wadding was used for the older child and the 4oz. wadding for the younger child.

### Materials

80cm (⅞yd) of 90cm wide (36in) top fabric (yellow).
80cm (⅞yd) of 90cm wide (36in) lining fabric (turquoise).
80cm (⅞yd) of 90cm wide (36in) 2oz. wadding (padding).

7 metres (7¾yd) of 3mm wide polyester crépe ribbon (red).
50cm (½yd) of 90cm wide 36in) contrasting fabric for binding the edges.
30cm (¼yd) of 55mm (2¼in) wide red ribbon for appliqué.
Matching thread to ribbon.
2 packets of red ring tops.
Small piece of bondaweb for appliqué.
Dressmaker's graph paper and pencil.

## Order of Work

### Pattern

**1** Enlarge pattern pieces. Add a seam allowance on sleeve underarm seam only. All other edges are bound with a bias trimming so no extra seam is necessary.

**2** To cut out the fabric, wadding and lining, refold the fabrics following the layout in the diagram (*fig. 1*). Cut one bodice section on the folded fabric and the two sleeve sections on the single fabric. Cut out the top fabric, the lining and the wadding. Do not cut down the centre front of the jacket at this stage.

**3** Cut out contrasting fabric on the bias grain into 5cm (2in) strips measuring 2½ metres (2¾yd) long when together to make the binding for the edging.

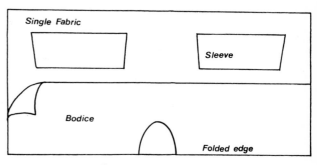

Fig 1

## Appliqué

**1** Mark the position of the longest diagonal ribbon on the top fabric only with a water-erasable pen. Mark the position of the other ribbons 7cm (2¾in) apart until the top fabric is covered (eleven quilting lines altogether) (*fig. 2*). Mark the position of the ribbons on both of the sleeves 7cm (2¾in) apart and 7cm (2¾in) in from cuff edge (*fig. 3*).

**2** Press bondaweb on to the back of the wide ribbon and draw three half-circles for the bird's head by tracing off the diagram (*fig. 4*). Cut out the appliqué shapes in both ribbon and fabric.

**3** Place the large circles on to the bird's head and the smaller circles inside the large circles. Press to bond into place.

**4** Position the bird's heads on to the jacket (*fig. 2*) and press again to bond in place. Machine around the edge of the appliqué with a number two close satin stitch, and around the eyes to hold in position and eliminate fraying. Press. (The beak is stitched in place after the quilting is completed.)

**Appliqué Design**

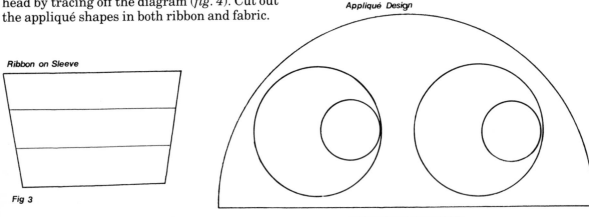

Fig 4

**Ribbon on Sleeve**

Fig 3

Fig 2

**Position of Ribbon for Quilting & Appliqué**

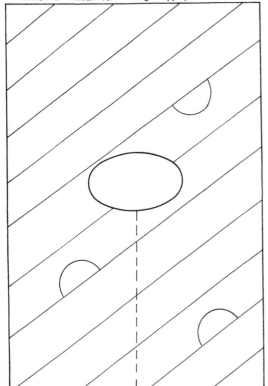

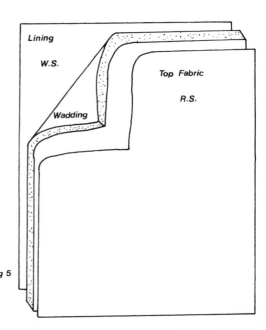

Lining

W.S.

Top Fabric

R.S.

Wadding

Fig 5

## Quilting

Iron both the top fabric and the lining thoroughly before tacking them together for quilting.

**1** Place wadding onto the wrong side of lining, and top fabric onto wadding (*fig. 5*).

**2** Tack these three layers together carefully, starting at your centre back neck and working down towards your hem and out towards the sides, until the three layers are sandwiched smoothly together.

**3** Repeat this process for both of the sleeves.

**4** Fit the embroidery foot into the machine.

**5** Machine the first ribbon in position along the longest diagonal line with a small zig-zag stitch the width of the ribbon.

**6** Complete the ribbon quilting following your guide lines 7cm (2¾in) apart until the rectangle is covered. Machine each row of ribbon in the same direction to eliminate any wrinkles in the quilting.

**7** Quilt the sleeves with two bands of ribbon 7cm (2¾in) apart.

**8** Place the bird's beak in position 3mm (⅛in) over the narrow ribbon and between the eyes. Machine in position with a close satin stitch set at number 2.

## Making up the jacket

**1** Bind hem and top edge of sleeves with the contrasting bias trimming, trim ends and press carefully over binding only.

**2** Bind the side seams of the jacket in the same way, pressing carefully when complete. The binding can be hand-sewn on the wrong side or machine-stitched for speed by stitching in the ditch, i.e. by machining between bodice and binding.

**3** Place jacket on a flat surface with sleeve edges butting edges of jacket and align balance marks. Mark the position of the first ring top on the shoulder line on both jacket and sleeve. Mark two more either side of this line, five altogether (*fig. 7*), and 6cm (2¼in) apart. Fit the top stud in the jacket first, check the fitting again for base and fit the base stud.

**4** Separate the jacket fronts by cutting down the centre front line from neck to hem (*fig. 7*).

**5** Machine underarms seams in the sleeves with a flat fell seam stitch on your normal seamline. Trim the inner seam allowance to 3mm (⅛in) and trim away the wadding. Turn under 6mm (¼in) on your seam edge and stitch the folded edge to the garment (*fig. 6*).

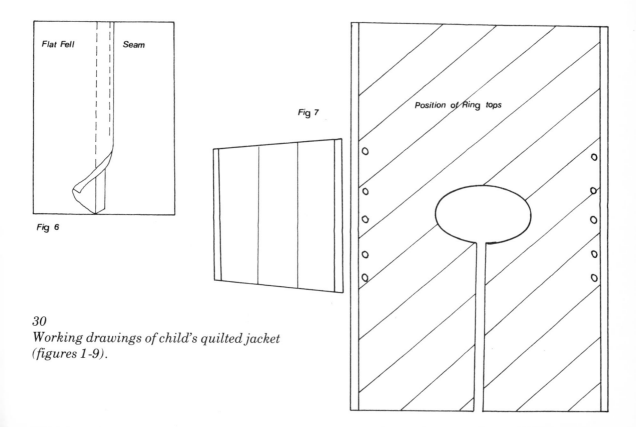

Flat Fell    Seam

*Fig 6*

Fig 7

Position of Ring tops

30
*Working drawings of child's quilted jacket (figures 1-9).*

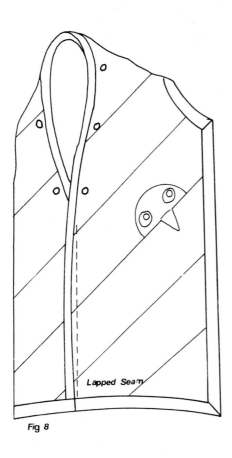

Fig 8

**6** Place side seams of the jacket together by lapping the front edges over the back edges. Pin back and machine in position by stitching in the ditch, between the jacket and binding, up to the balance marks (*fig. 8*). (Check this length; you may wish to leave more opening for the sleeve.)

**7** Bind jacket along the hem, front edges and neck edge, starting and finishing at the side seam. Align seams of binding to overlap on the jacket side seams.

**8** Pop sleeves into place in jacket and turn back cuff.

**9** Make fastenings for the centre front with the narrow ribbon or a rouleau strip, by making into a Chinese ball button and loop fastening.

**10** To make the Chinese ball buttons and loops follow the diagrams (*fig. 31*) and hand-sew in place as shown in figures 5 and 6.

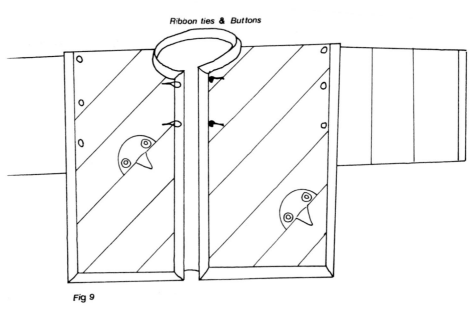

Fig 9

52

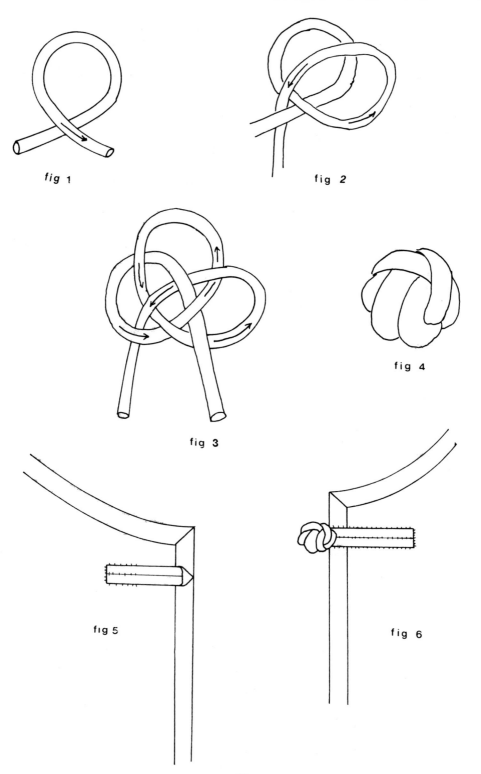

fig 1

fig 2

fig 3

fig 4

fig 5

fig 6

31
*Chinese ball button for child's quilted jacket
(figures 1-6).*

32
*Back view of child's quilted jacket. Showing the
appliqué work. The ribbons worn by the children
are a woven Swiss viscose jacquard.*

# An evening gown

This lovely evening gown (*colour plate 6 and 7*) was made in a textured pure silk and was lined throughout in silk. The small stand collar, cuffs and shoulder line are woven in a matching 10mm ribbon, on the bias grain. The gown has a slashed front neckline and deep cut-away back neck, fastened with small rouleau loops and buttons. The sleeve is open from shoulder to wrist and closed with a small plastic press stud. The skirt is pleated on to a slightly-bloused bodice. Small rouleau bows decorate the back neck and cuffs.

The measurements given for the pattern will fit sizes 12 to 14. Size 12: Bust 90cm (35½in). Waist 69cm (27in). Nape to waist 42cm (16½in) + 4cm blousing.

## Materials
4 metres (4½yd) of 115cm-wide (45in) silk or synthetic crepe de chine.
4 metres (4½yd) of 115cm-wide (45in) lining fabric.
12 metres (13yd) of 10mm-wide matching single-faced satin ribbon.
50cm (20in) of lightweight iron-on interfacing.
Matching sewing thread.
Dressmaker graph paper and pencil.
Five 7mm plastic press studs for collar and cuff and waistband closure.
80cm x 2.5cm (1yd x 1in) polyester skirt petersham and large hook and bar for fastening inside waist.
Seven 11mm easy-cover buttons.
This gown was lined throughout but, depending on fabric used, this is not always necessary (although the sleeves must be lined).

## Pattern
Enlarge the pattern pieces and add on a seam allowance of 1½cm (⅝in) on all pieces.

*33*
*Evening gown.*

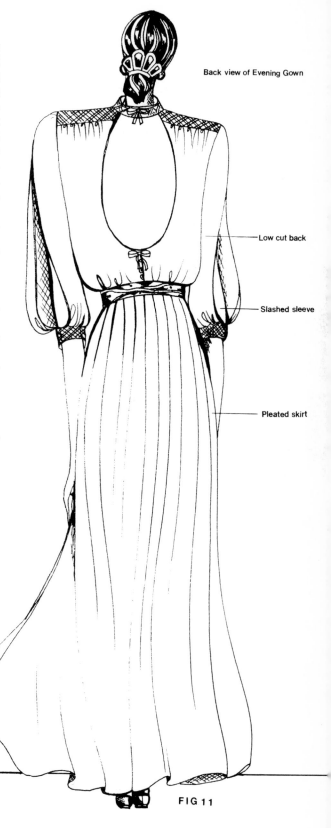

Back view of Evening Gown

Low cut back

Slashed sleeve

Pleated skirt

FIG 11

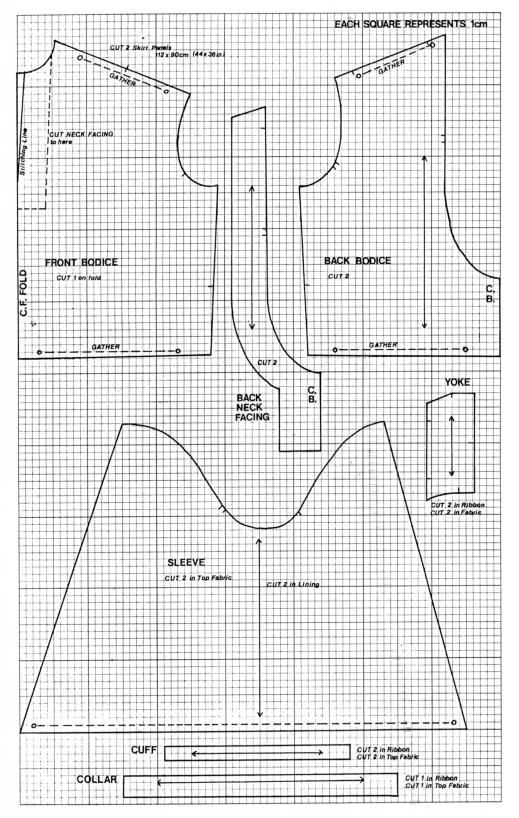

EACH SQUARE REPRESENTS 1cm

CUT 2 Skirt Panels
112 x 90cm (44 x 36 in)

GATHER

GATHER

CUT NECK FACING
to here

Stitching Line

FRONT BODICE

CUT 1 on fold

C.F. FOLD

GATHER

BACK BODICE

CUT 2

GATHER

C.
B.

CUT 2

BACK
NECK
FACING

C.
B.

YOKE

CUT 2 in Ribbon
CUT 2 in Fabric

SLEEVE

CUT 2 in Top Fabric

CUT 2 in Lining

CUFF

CUT 2 in Ribbon
CUT 2 in Top Fabric

COLLAR

CUT 1 in Ribbon
CUT 1 in Top Fabric

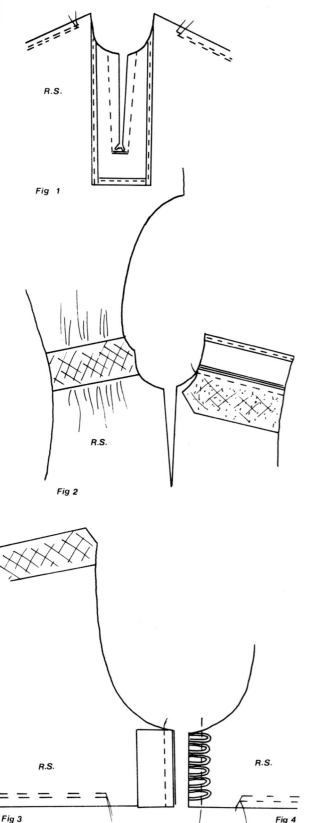

**Fig 1**

R.S.

**Fig 2**

R.S.

**Fig 3**

R.S.

R.S.

**Fig 4**

### Ribbon weaving

Weave the two yoke sections, one collar section and two cuff sections, following the instructions for the bias weave on page *17*. Cut out these pieces in the ribbon weaving and machine all round the edge just inside the seam allowance to to hold the ribbons in place.

### Making up: order of work

**1** With fabric folded in half lengthwise, cut out two skirt panels (check your skirt length) 112cm x 90cm (44in x 36in). Cut out all the pattern pieces, checking that the arrows follow the lengthwise grain of fabric. Cut out the lining in the same way. Cut fabric for seven rouleau loops 2cm x 20cm (¾in x 8in) on the bias grain, and a button extension 6cm x 12cm (2½in x 5in). If lining is used, tack it to the front and back bodice and work as if it were one fabric.

*Facings*

**2** Turn under 6mm (¼in) on the outside edge of the front and back facings.

**3** With right sides together, pin the front facing to the centre front line and machine along the stitching line. Slash between the stitching and clip into the corners. Turn the facing to the inside and press. Tack across the neck (*fig. 1*).

**4** Gather the upper edges of front and back bodice between the balance marks, with two rows of long stitches.

*Yokes*

**5** Pin the two ribbon yoke sections to the upper edges of the front bodice, adjust gathers.

**6** Turn in the seam allowance on the back edge of the yoke facing. Press.

**7** Pin the right side of the yoke facing to the wrong side of the front bodice; machine together. Trim the seam. Turn the yokes up. Press (*fig. 2*)

**8** Pin the yoke to the back bodice, adjust gathers and machine in place; trim. Press the seams up. Hand sew the facing to the seamline.

*Button extension and rouleau loops*

**9** With right sides together fold the fabric in half lengthways and machine across the top edge. Turn to the right side and press. Pin to the left side of the centre back edge (*fig. 3*). Make seven rouleau loops on the right side of the centre back and machine in place just inside the seam allowance (*fig. 4*).

### Back facing

**10** With right sides together pin the facing to the back bodice: from the ribbon yoke, along the curved edge and down the centre back over the button extension and rouleau loops. Machine in place. Trim the seam, clip the curve and corners (*fig. 5*). Turn to the right side. Edge stitch as far as possible along the curve. Press (*fig. 6*).

### Collar

**11** Tack and press the hem on one edge of the facing. Pin the facing to the collar and machine across both ends and along the unnotched edge. Trim seams, turn to the right side and press.

**12** Pin the collar to the neck edge, matching balance marks. [The collar is attached to the bodice across the front and half of the yoke only, as the back is cut away (*fig. 7*).] Machine in place. Trim; clip around the curve. Press the seam up into the collar. Keeping the collar band the same width, turn in the hem on both collar and facing and hand sew into place.

### Cuff

**13** Make up the cuff following the instructions for the turquoise suit.

### Sleeve

**14** With the right sides together, pin and machine the sleeve lining along centre front and centre back lines only. Trim the seam. Turn to the right side and press. Tack along the sleeve head to hold the lining in position. Gather the lower edge of the sleeve with two rows of large machine stitches between balance points (*fig. 8*).

**15** Pin the cuff to the sleeve, adjusting gathers and leaving a 2.5cm (1in) extension on the back of the cuff. Machine in place. Trim the seam; press towards the cuff. Hand sew the facing to the seamline on the inside.

**16** Pin the sleeve into the armhole, being careful to match all balance marks (sleeve opening is 2.5cm (1in) from front yoke) in order for the sleeve to fall open at the right angle. Tack, then check that the sleeve is hanging correctly. Machine in place, machine again 6mm (¼in) away. Trim to 1cm (½in) to neaten the seam. Press the seam towards the sleeve.

**17** With right sides together, pin, tack and machine the bodice together at the side seams, with a flat seam. Neaten the seam and press open.

**18** Make two rows of gathering stitches between the balance points on the front and back bodice.

*Skirt* (2.5cm (1in) pleats all round and seams down centre front and centre back.)

**19** With right sides together, pin, tack and machine skirt panels together, leaving an opening of 22cm (8¾in) along the centre back seam. Press the seam open and neaten.

**20** Insert a zip in the centre back using the lapped method and hand-sew into place (*fig. 9*).

**21** Place the first pleat in the skirt just over the zip so that the pleat conceals it. (The right side of the back bodice will align with this.)

**22** Pleat the skirt all round, making sure centre front seam is concealed in the pleats. Reduce the skirt to fit your waist size by making the pleats larger or smaller. If pleats are preferred across the front and back only, then align with the gathers on bodice back and front. If the skirt is lined, make up the lining and with the wrong sides together tack the skirt and lining together around the waist.

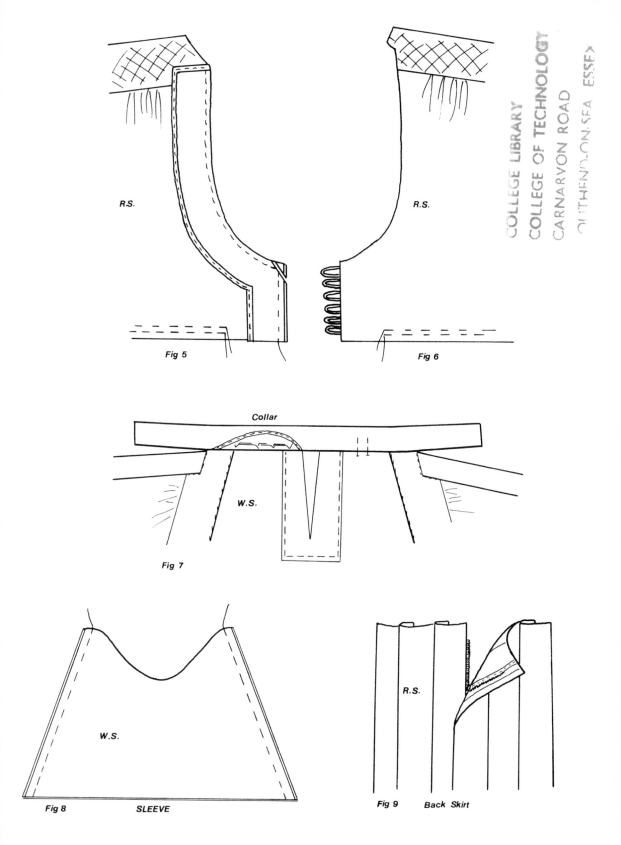

R.S.

R.S.

Fig 5

Fig 6

Collar

W.S.

Fig 7

W.S.

Fig 8         SLEEVE

R.S.

Fig 9     Back Skirt

59

*Attaching skirt to bodice*

**23** Pin the skirt to the bodice, align the centre back of the skirt with the seam of the button extension and lapped side of zip in line with the rouleau edge. Pin the centre front of the skirt with the centre front of the bodice, and align sides. Adjust the gathers on the bodice, tack and check the fitting. Machine in place. Trim the seam to 1cm. Neaten the seam and press up (*fig. 10*).

**24** Measure the petersham to fit your waist and attach a hook and bar to either end. Sew it down flat to the waist seam at centre front, sides and side back. This is to anchor the waistline and allow the bodice to blouse softly. Attach a length of elastic from inside the back facing to fit snugly across the front of the body and under the back facing again. This holds the deep neckline comfortably close to the skin.

**25** Check the hem and level off. Hand-sew in place.

*Finishing*

**26** Sew 7mm plastic press studs to the cuffs, collar band and top and bottom of the inner edge of the button extension (*fig. 10*). With the rouleau, make three bows for decoration at the back neck and cuffs, each measuring 30cm (12in).

## Cummerband

A 5cm (2in) wide gold lamé cummerband was made for the waistline and small gold beads were scattered over it, each held in place with a single stitch.

*Materials*

Cut a 5cm-wide (2in) piece of pelmet vilene the length of your waist plus an 8cm (3in) wrap-over piece. Cut gold lamé 18cm (7in) wide and long enough to cover the interfacing plus a 1cm (⅜in) seam allowance all round.

*Making the cummerbund*

Enclose the interfacing in the fabric with a 1cm (⅜in) seam along the lower edge. Keeping the back of your cummerbund flat, gather the excess fabric on to the front cummerbund only and pin folds of fabric into a random design. Fold the gathered ends of the cummerbund under the flat backing and hand-sew in place. Stitch the beads in a random design to hold the pleats in place. Mark the positions for fastening and close with two skirt hooks and bars.

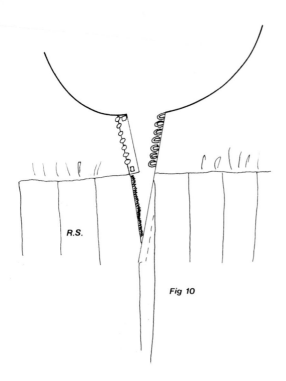

R.S.

Fig 10

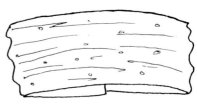

FIG II

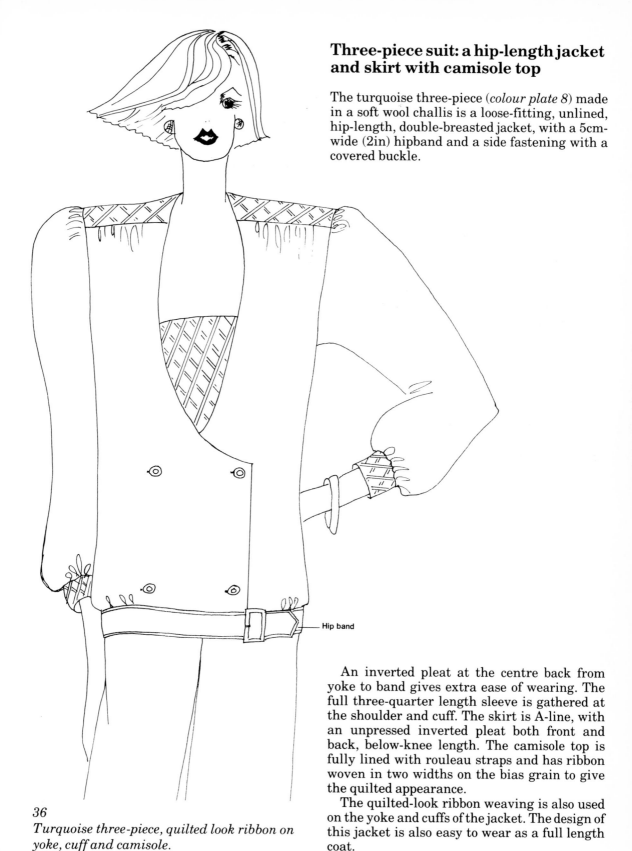

## Three-piece suit: a hip-length jacket and skirt with camisole top

The turquoise three-piece (*colour plate 8*) made in a soft wool challis is a loose-fitting, unlined, hip-length, double-breasted jacket, with a 5cm-wide (2in) hipband and a side fastening with a covered buckle.

Hip band

An inverted pleat at the centre back from yoke to band gives extra ease of wearing. The full three-quarter length sleeve is gathered at the shoulder and cuff. The skirt is A-line, with an unpressed inverted pleat both front and back, below-knee length. The camisole top is fully lined with rouleau straps and has ribbon woven in two widths on the bias grain to give the quilted appearance.

The quilted-look ribbon weaving is also used on the yoke and cuffs of the jacket. The design of this jacket is also easy to wear as a full length coat.

36
*Turquoise three-piece, quilted look ribbon on yoke, cuff and camisole.*

61

*Pattern for turquoise three-piece.*

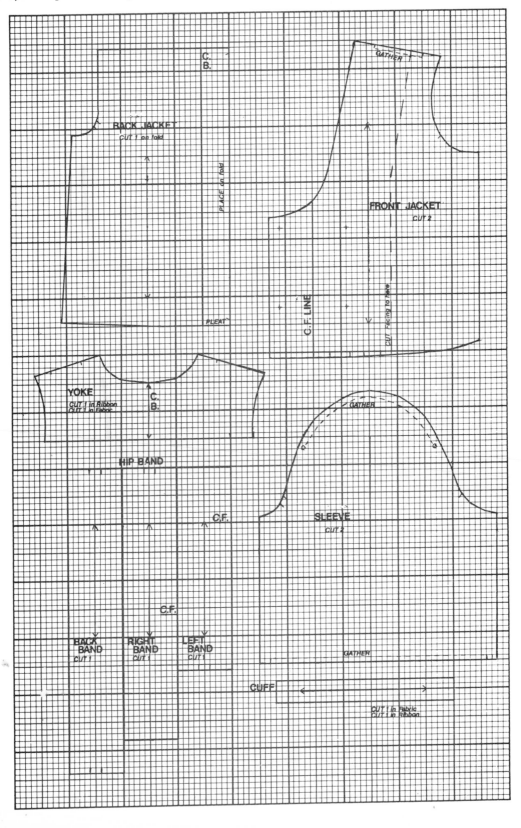

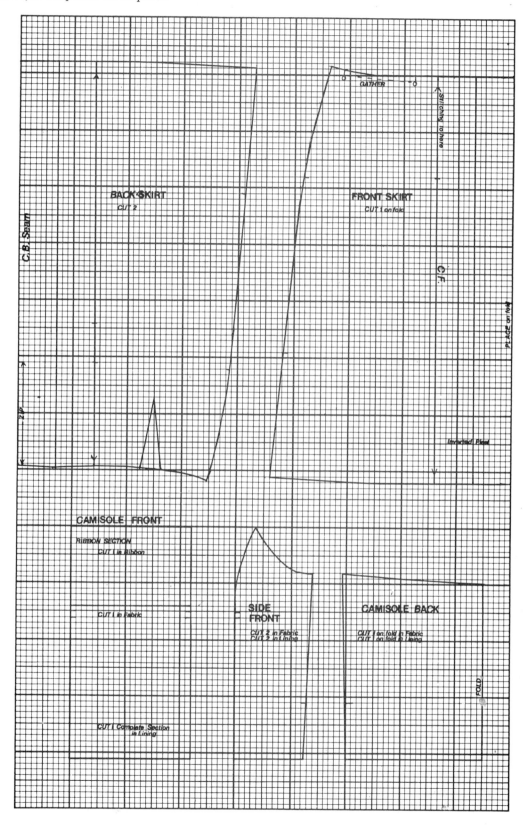

## Materials

To fit: bust size 92cm (36in); hip 97 – 102cm (38 – 40in).

3 metres (3¼yd) wool challis/wool crepe, 150cm (60in) wide.

1 metre (¾yd) lining for skirt, 150cm (60in) wide.

15 metres (16¼yd) of 10mm-wide single-faced satin ribbon in matching colour.

15 metres (16¼yd) of 3mm-wide single-faced satin ribbon for yoke and cuff, in matching colour.

Iron-on lightweight interfacing.

Matching sewing thread.

20cm (8in) zip for skirt, plus hook and eye for waistband.

Four 15mm easy-cover buttons.

One 30mm x 40mm easy-cover buckle.

50cm (20in) of 6mm-wide (¼in) elastic for back of camisole.

## Pattern

Enlarge the pattern pieces [each square represents 1cm (³⁄₈in)] and add on a seam allowance of 1½cm (⅝in) on all pieces.

## Making up: order of work

*Yoke*

**1** Weave one yoke section and two cuff sections, following the instructions for the 'quilted bias weave' on page 17. Cut out the yoke and cuffs.

*Jacket*

**2** Make an inverted pleat at the centre back of the jacket, by tacking along the centre back line. Stitch the top and hem to a depth of 4cm (1½in). Place the fold of the fabric along the centre back line to form an inverted pleat. Press.

**3** On the front jacket at shoulder line, make two rows of gathering stitches between the balance marks.

**4** With right sides together and raw edges aligned, pin and tack the ribbon yoke to the front and back sections of the jacket. Adjust gathers on the front shoulder (*fig. 1*) and

machine in place. Trim the seam. Press seams towards the shoulder.

**5** Apply the interfacing to the wrong side of the front jacket facing. Turn in the hem along the straight edge, machine in place and trim to 6mm (¼in). Press.

**6** Pin, tack and machine the jacket facing to the yoke facing at shoulder line, trim the seam and press open.

**7** With right sides together, pin this facing around the neck and front edges of the jacket (*fig. 2*). Tack and machine in place. Trim the seam allowance, clip the curve around neck and front; this will enable the facing to lie flat when turned to the inside.

**8** Extend the facing and seam allowance of the neck and front edge from the right side, understitch close to the seamline, around the neck and along the curved edge as far as possible. Turn the facing to the inside. Make sure the edge of the seam lies just inside the jacket. Press carefully. On the lower edge of the yoke facing, turn in the raw edge and hand sew to the yoke.

**9** With right sides together, stitch the jacket together at the sides with a machine fell seam. Press flat.

*Sleeve*

**10** Stitch the seam allowance in the sleeve with a machine fell seam, leaving open 4cm (1½in) from the cuff edge. Press. Turn under raw edges and machine them flat (*fig. 3*). Press. Make two rows of gathering stitch along the lower edge, using large machine stitches. Gather the sleeve head between the balance points.

*Cuff*

**11** Turn in the seam allowance on the upper edge of the cuff facing sections. Tack and press. Trim to 6mm (¼in). With right sides together, pin the facing to the ribbon cuff sections, tack and machine it in place. Press the seam flat. Trim and layer the seam allowance (*fig. 4*). Taper corners. Turn the cuffs right side out. Roll the facing edges slightly under and press.

*38*
*Working drawings for turquoise three-piece (figures 1-16).*

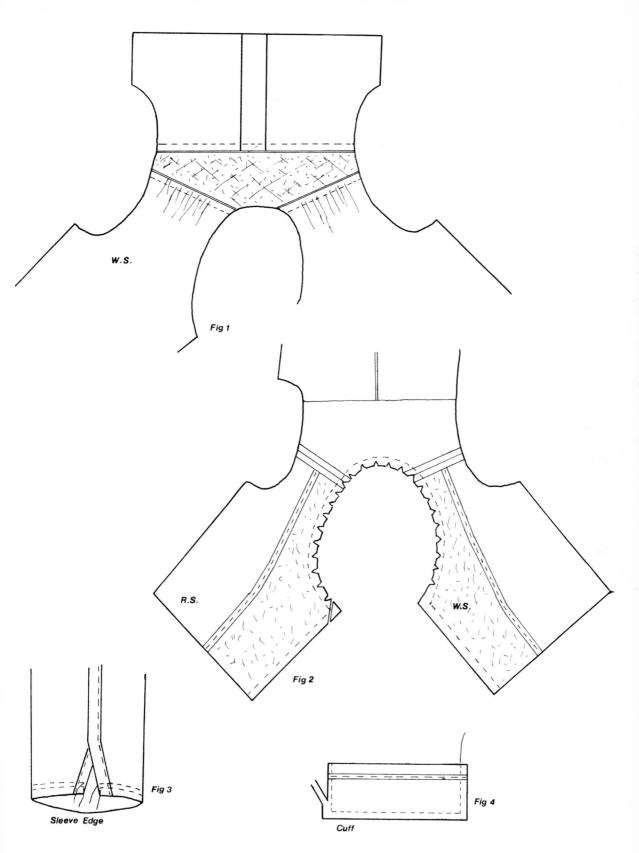

W.S.

Fig 1

R.S.

W.S.

Fig 2

Fig 3

Sleeve Edge

Fig 4

Cuff

65

**12** Pin the cuff to the sleeve, adjusting gathers and leaving a 3cm (1¼in) overlap on the cuff as shown. Tack and machine. Trim the seam allowance. Press the seam towards the cuff. On the inside, slip stitch the tacked edge over the seam (*fig. 5*).

**13** Pin the sleeve into the armhole adjusting gathers, tack and machine in place. Machine again 6mm (¼in) away, trim the seam to 1cm (⅜in). Press the sleeve seam very carefully, with seam towards sleeve, do not press the gathers.

*Hip Band*
**14** Apply the interfacing to the wrong side of the hip band. With right sides together, machine the hip band at the side seams with a flat seam. Trim and press seam open (*fig. 6*).

**15** Fold the band in half, lengthways with right sides together, stitch along the top of the right band extension and left band front edge (*fig. 7*). Trim seam, clip corners and turn right extension through to the right side. Clip to the machine stitches.

**16** Following the balance marks, make three small pleats in the lower edge of the jacket, facing towards side seams (*fig. 8*). Pin and tack the band in place, adjusting to fit. Machine in place. Trim seam. Press the seam down into the band. On the inside, tack the raw edge over the seam. Top stitch the band all round close to the edge and a second row 6mm (¼in) away. Press.

*Skirt*
**17** Tack along the centre front line and centre back line from the top edge to the hem and along the back seam. Machine down centre front line 18cm (7in) and along centre back line between balance marks (*fig. 9*). Press the stitching. Place the front fold to centre front line to form an inverted pleat. Press only 18cm (7in) from the top edge, as this is an unpressed pleat. (It could be made into a pressed pleat if you wish.) Press the back skirt in the same way, i.e. to the end of the stitches (and along back seam from balance points) (*fig. 10*).

**18** Make darts in the back skirt and fit the zip. On the front skirt make two rows of gathering between balance points. With right sides together, pin and tack the skirt together at side seams, check the fitting and machine with a flat seam. Press. Make up the lining, omitting the back pleat; with wrong sides together, tack the lining into the skirt around the top edge.

*Waistband*
**19** Cut the waistband to fit your waist measurement plus a 5cm (2in) overlap x 8.5cm (3½in) wide. Interface. Top stitch all around (*fig. 11*).

**20** Pin the waistband to the skirt, right sides together. Adjust ease and gathers on the front, and leaving an overlap on the right side of the zip, tack together. Try it on for fit. Machine and trim the seam. Press the seam towards the waistband. Turn under the raw edge inside the band and hand-sew to the seam (*fig. 12*).

**21** Level the hem and finish by hand, or machine finish to match the hip band.

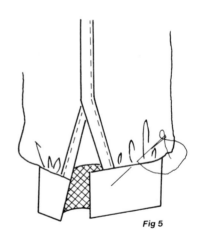

Fig 5

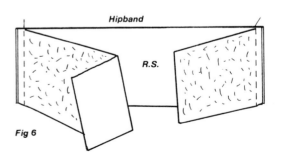

Hipband

R.S.

Fig 6

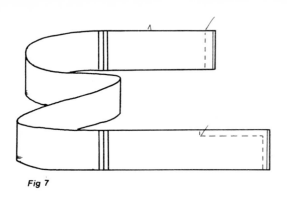

Fig 7

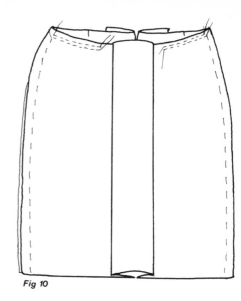

Fig 10

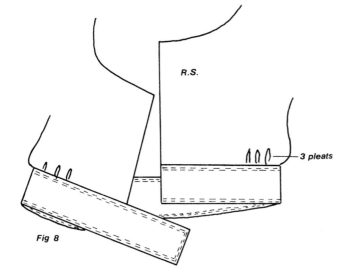

R.S.

3 pleats

Fig 8

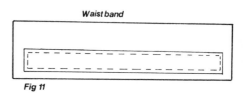

Waist band

Fig 11

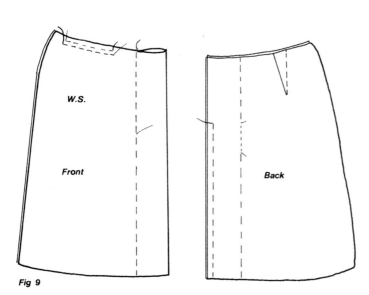

W.S.

Front

Back

Fig 9

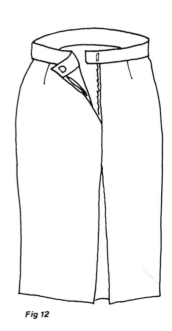

Fig 12

*Camisole top*

**22** Make up the ribbon weaving for the top edge and cut to measure 23cm x 14cm (9in x 5½in).

**23** Pin, tack and machine the centre front panel to the ribbon weaving section (*fig. 13*). Trim Press the seam up.

**24** With right sides together and raw edges aligned, pin, tack and machine the centre front panel to the side fronts, trim and seam and press towards the side seams. (This is to allow the ribbon section to lie flat.)

**25** With right sides facing, place the back and front of the camisole together (*fig. 14*). Pin, tack and machine the side seams together. Trim and press them open.

**26** Cut two bias strips for the straps 53cm x 4cm (21in x 1½in) and fold them in half lengthways. Stitch down the centre, trim slightly (not too much otherwise the rouleau will look like string). Turn through and press.

**27** Place the straps in position, i.e. each side of the front panel and 11.5cm (4½in) in from the side seam towards the back. Adjust to fit.

**28** Make up the camisole lining and, with right sides together, pin, tack and machine all round the top edge (*fig. 15*). Trim and seam, snip the underarm curve. Turn the lining to the wrong side. Roll the edges until the join is showing slightly on the inside and straps are extended. Press.

**29** Machine along the top edge of the back camisole and again 1cm (⅜in) away. Cut 36cm (14in) of elastic and, using a bodkin, thread through the rows of machining (fig. 16). Adjust to fit. Sew securely into the side seam. Finish the hemline on the camisole and lining either by hand or machine.

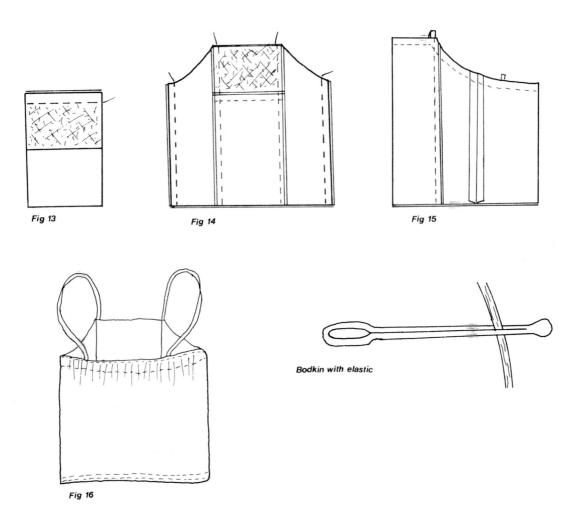

Fig 13

Fig 14

Fig 15

Fig 16

*Bodkin with elastic*

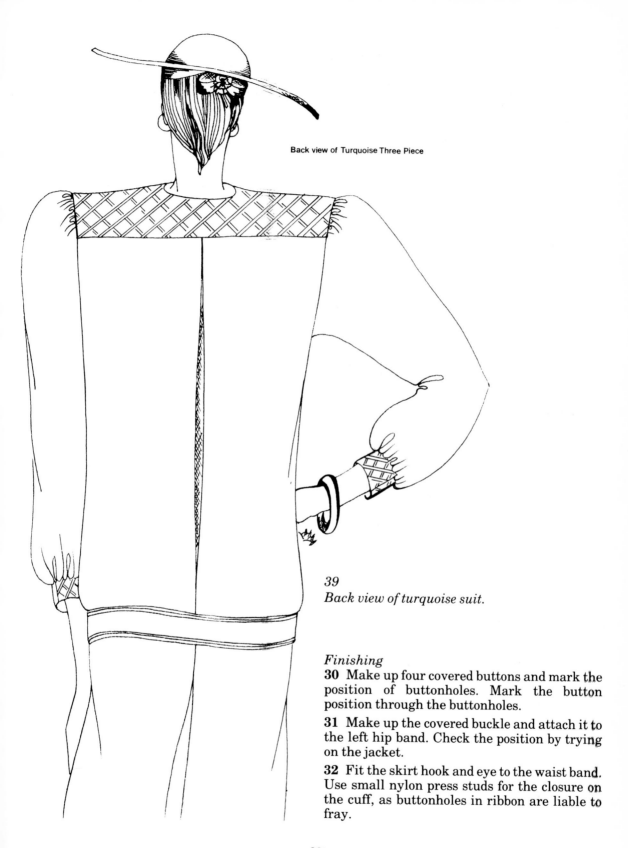

Back view of Turquoise Three Piece

*39*
*Back view of turquoise suit.*

### Finishing

**30** Make up four covered buttons and mark the position of buttonholes. Mark the button position through the buttonholes.

**31** Make up the covered buckle and attach it to the left hip band. Check the position by trying on the jacket.

**32** Fit the skirt hook and eye to the waist band. Use small nylon press studs for the closure on the cuff, as buttonholes in ribbon are liable to fray.

40
*Pure silk jacket with shoulder yoke using two widths of ribbon. This is included as an alternative style of jacket for those with some dressmaking experience and who can therefore adapt patterns for different styles.*

## Sleeveless velvet jacket

This velvet jacket was decorated with the narrow ribbon – using the shuttle technique – working therefore with the wrong side of the garment facing you and the design reversed.

The instructions here are for the sleeveless jacket, but the pattern can also be used for the fingertip version with sleeves, illustrated here (*colour plate 11*).

For the sleeveless pattern, cut the sleeve facings to the dotted line and to the jacket length for the short version.

### Materials
To fit: bust size approx. 92cm (36in)
60cm (¾yd) velvet or fabric of your choice, 150cm (60in) wide.
60cm (¾yd) synthetic 2oz wadding.
60cm (¾yd) lining fabric 150cm (60in) wide.
6 metres (6½yd.) of 1.5mm-wide ribbon for shuttle embroidery.
50cm (½yd) of 35mm and 50mm-wide ribbon for appliqué.
Sewing thread to match ribbon.
Paper for pattern and a pencil.
Lightweight iron-on interfacing.

### Pattern and preparation
**1** Enlarge the pattern pieces and add a 1½cm (⅝in) seam allowance on all sections.

**2** Cut out front and back in the fabric, wadding and lining. Cut out the facing in the top fabric only.

**3** Place the wadding onto the wrong side of the velvet and tack all over to keep it in place, thoroughly smoothing the fabric while tacking.

Sleeveless Velvet Jacket

Ribbon Embroidery

*41*
*Sleeveless velvet jacket.*

71

## 42

*Pattern for velvet jacket.*

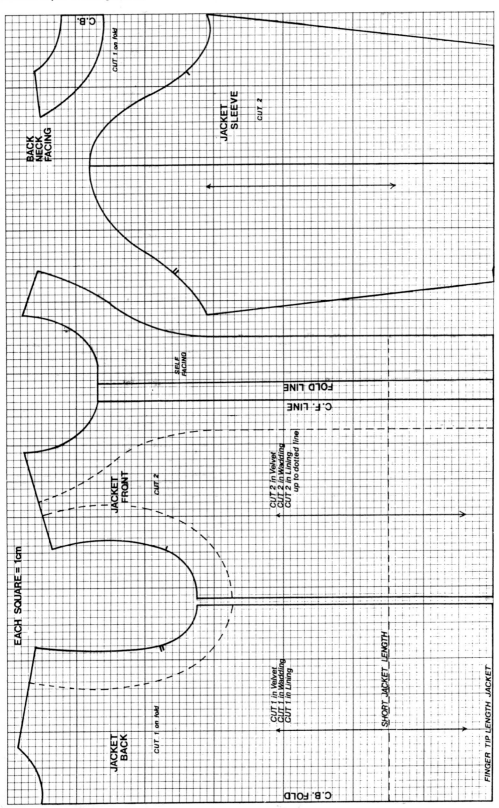

*12. This burgundy shirt illustrates the bias weave using 10mm and 3mm wide ribbon. For this effect, use one 10mm ribbon and four 3mm wide ribbons alternately across the weaving.*

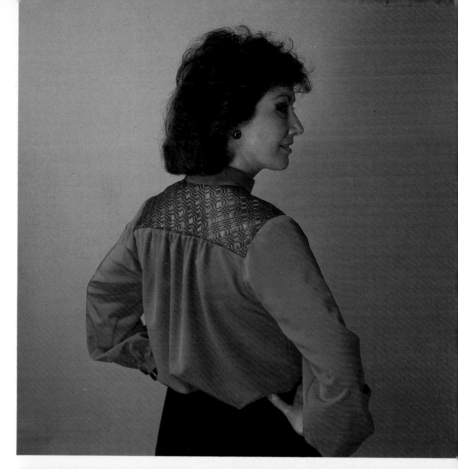

*13. Knitting with ribbon: Mohair and ribbon sweater. The ribbon used here for this slash-neck top sweater is 100% polyester. The sweater is hand knitted in two shades of mohair with mixed fibres. (Jose Walker).*

14. *Ribbon-laced sweater.
(Christina Veekman).*

15. *Evening purse with
plaited shoulder strap.*

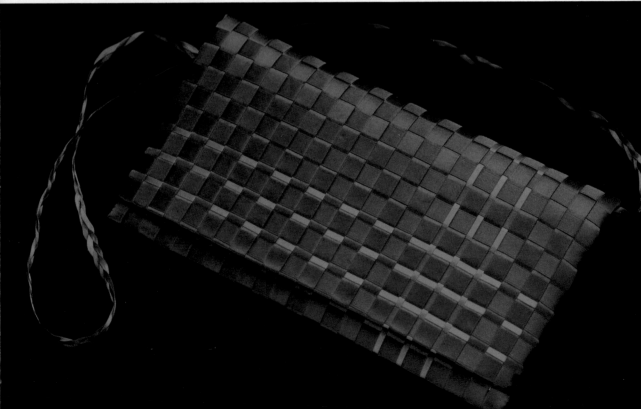

16. Travel coat.

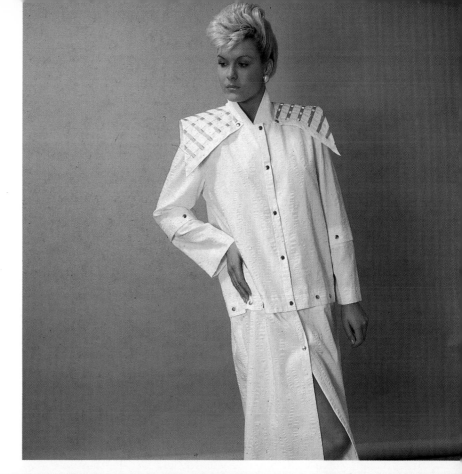

17. Epaulet of travel coat.

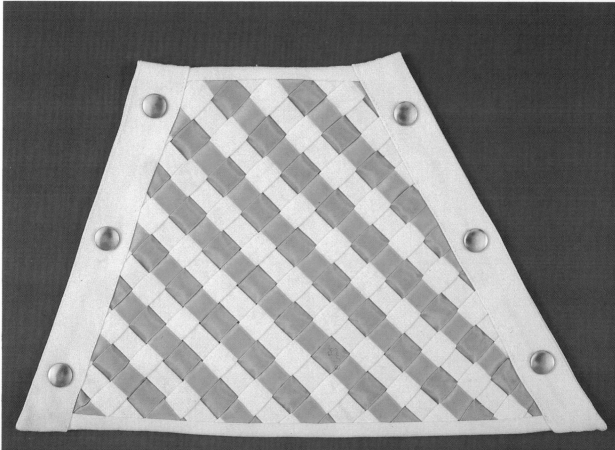

18. Patchwork quilt and pillow set.

19. Close-up showing detail of ribbon weaving and fabric and ribbon in the bed quilt and pillow.

*Working the design*

**4** Machine together the shoulder seams and trim away the wadding as close as possible to the machine stitches, to reduce bulk.

**5** Press seams open (*fig. 1*). Draw your design for ribbon embroidery onto the wadding with a water-erasable pen, using figure 1 as a rough guide. Work all machining in the same direction to prevent the fabric wrinkling.

**6** Measure roughly the amount of ribbon you will use for each line across the jacket (approx. 2 metres (2¼yd)) and wind this by hand or machine onto your bobbin, loosen the tension screw in the bobbin case to allow the ribbon to be pulled through, but still keeping a firm tension, use machine stitch length of 3mm (⅛in). Starting at the front left-hand side, with the wrong side of the work facing you, carefully machine from side front, over the shoulder and down across the back, finishing at side back. It is very important that each row is stitched in one operation as it would be very difficult to join the ribbon and this could look unsightly anyway, so do check the length of ribbon in your bobbin before you machine the next row.

**7** Rewind your bobbin with ribbon and machine the second row in the same way, following your drawn-out design. Now complete the last row, still working from left-hand front, over shoulder to lower back. You can put in more rows of machining if you wish.

**8** When the machining is complete, take out the tacking around the ribbon, but leave tacks in around the edge of the jacket, keeping the three layers of fabric together.

## Appliqué

**9** Using wide ribbon for appliqué, press the iron-on interfacing to the wrong side of the ribbon, and taking a line down the centre of the leaf, draw two halves of the motif on to the ribbon. Cut them out.

**10** Place the two halves together to form a whole leaf and tack or fuse it in position on the jacket, following the diagram as a rough guide.

**11** Machine along the edge of the leaf with a medium straight stitch and then zig-zag satin stitch to cover raw edges, and down the centre of the leaf to cover the join.

*Making up*

**12** Join side seams. Press open.

**13** Machine together the front neck facing to the back neck at shoulder seams (*fig. 2*). Press open.

43

*Working drawing for velvet jacket (figures 1-6).*

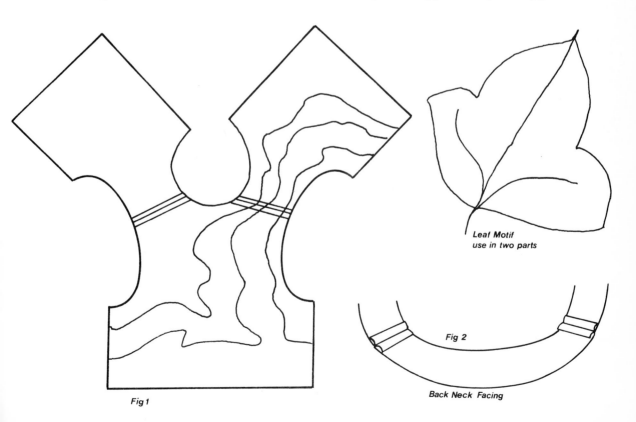

Leaf Motif
use in two parts

Fig 2

Back Neck Facing

Fig 1

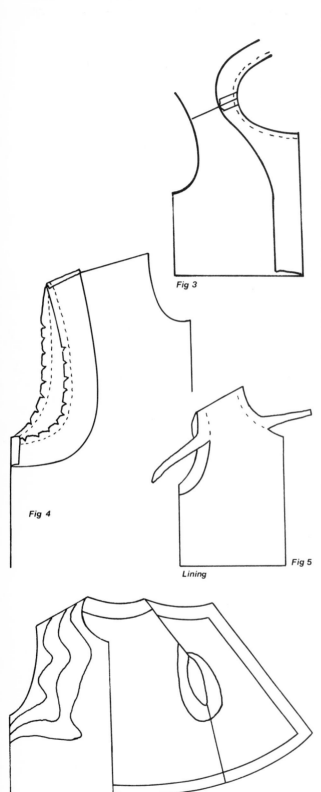

Fig 3

Fig 4

Lining

Fig 5

Fig 6

**14** Pin the neck facing in position (*fig. 3*). Tack and machine along the neckline edge. Trim seams in layers and clip curves. Turn to the inside and tack the facing, rolling the seam line slightly inside the jacket. Press.

**15** With right sides together, machine the armhole facing at shoulder and underarm. Press the seams open and trim to half width.

**16** With right sides together, pin and tack the facing to the jacket armhole, matching shoulder and underarm seams. Machine and press flat.

**17** Trim and layer the seam allowances; clip into them to enable the facing to lie flat when turned out (*fig. 4*).

**18** Turn the facing to the inside and roll the seam line slightly inside (as with neck facing). Align the shoulder and underarm seams, sew facing to backing. Turn the hem 3cm (1¼in) at the lower edges.

**19** Using the back and front patterns only, cut out the lining. With right sides together, machine side seams. Trim and press open.

**20** Trim 1cm (⅜in) away from the armhole edge and neck edge of the lining (*fig. 5*).

**21** Lay the inside of the lining to the inside of the jacket, align side seams and tack in position. Working on a flat surface, smooth the lining to the left front facing, turn under the seam allowance [roughly 1cm (⅜in) seam] and tack in position. Do the same on the right front.

**22** Smooth the lining out over the back of the jacket and tack round armhole edges and neck line; turn the seam allowance under, so that roughly 2.5cm (1in) of facing is showing around the neck edge, armhole and front edges.

**23** Hand-sew the shoulder seams together.

**24** Make a small fold in the bottom hemline for ease of wear.

**25** Hand-sew the lining all around the edges (*fig. 6*). Press carefully. If you should experience any difficulty using the shuttle technique with the narrow ribbon, it is possible to work from the right side of the jacket and to couch the ribbon in place with a medium-sized zig-zag stitch.

To do this, draw your random design on the right side of your jacket, and using the satin stitch foot on your machine and a sewing thread to match the ribbon, feed the narrow ribbon under the foot and towards the back of the machine. Place your jacket under the machine and this time starting from your right side lower back, lower the foot and machine with the ribbon in the centre of the foot, continuing the zig-zag stitch across the back, over the shoulder and down the front left-hand side of the jacket in one continuous operation. Stitch the other two rows in the same way. Press each row as you work very carefully and from the wrong side.

Look at the dressing gown (*fig. 45*) and dress and jacket (*fig. 46*) for more ideas on ribbon embroidery and appliqué.

*44*
*Illustration of embroidered jacket with long sleeves.*

Narrow ribbon Embroidery

Finger Tip Length Jacket

**45**
*The dressing gown was made from a commercial pattern and three different widths of ribbon were used to decorate it.*

*46*
*Dress and jacket with narrow ribbon embroidery using the shuttle technique. On the jacket, the ends of the narrow ribbon were used to embroider a small motif.*

## Shirt-dress with plain weave yoke and cuffs

This is a very easy design for most people to wear, and certainly a very comforable one. It is made here in navy blue wool challis, and is suitable for sizes 10-14.

The front and back are pleated into the lined ribbon woven yoke and fastened down the centre front with fabric-covered buttons.

Both the front band and stand collar are top stitched with two rows of stitching. Pockets are in the side seams. A narrow belt is threaded through the channel waist, tied at centre front and is finished with two rows of top stitching. The full-length sleeve has eleven small pleats set into ribbon-woven cuffs. A design which suits most figure types, it would look very good as an evening dress made to ankle or floor length. If preferred it could also be made without any casing at the waistline, and worn straight or belted with a purchased belt.

Although the yoke and cuffs here are worked in simple plain weave using three colours of ribbon, in fact any combination of weave is suitable. Either soft or crisp fabrics can be used to make the dress, e.g. wool crépe, lightweight double knits, lightweight flannel, challis or, for evening wear, the synthetic crépe de chine.

### Materials

2 metres 40cm (2¾yd) wool challis, 150cm (60in) wide for a short dress.
2 metres 80cm (3yd) fabric, 115cm (45in) wide for a short dress.
3 metres 40cm (3⅝yd) fabric, 115cm (45in) wide for a long dress.
5 metres (5½yd) of 10mm-wide single-faced satin ribbon in navy.
5 metres (5½yd) of 10mm-wide single-faced satin ribbon in silver.
5 metres (5½yd) of 10mm-wide single-faced satin ribbon in burgundy.
Lightweight iron-on interfacing.
14 easy-cover buttons.
Matching sewing thread.
2 small nylon snap fasteners.

### Pattern and preparation

Enlarge pattern pieces [each square equals 1cm (⅜in)] and add on seam allowance, 1½cm (⅝in) on all pieces, 4cm (1½in) on hem. Check back length measurement, skirt length and sleeve lengths and adjust to fit. There should be 4cm (1½in) blousing in bodice.

*Yoke*

Cut interfacing 48cm x 20cm (19in x 8in) and weave the ribbons in plain weave following instructions given in the 'Plain Weave' chapter. Cut out yoke, machine around edge of weaving to keep in shape. Press.

*Cuff*

The cuff is made with five widths of ribbon. The finished width of each cuff is three ribbons deep x 23cm (9in) long. To save time and ribbon, weave both cuffs simultaneously. To do this, cut ten lengths of ribbon 26cm (10in) in length and pin them on to the interfacing in colour sequence, leaving a 6mm (¼in) gap between ribbons 5 and 6; this enables you to separate them after weaving without cutting into the ribbon. Now complete the weaving, again in colour sequence. Press and separate the cuffs. Machine around the edge to hold them in place. Press again ready for use.

*47*
*Navy, burgundy and grey ribbons were used in plain weave to decorate this shirt dress.*

*Pattern for shirt dress.*

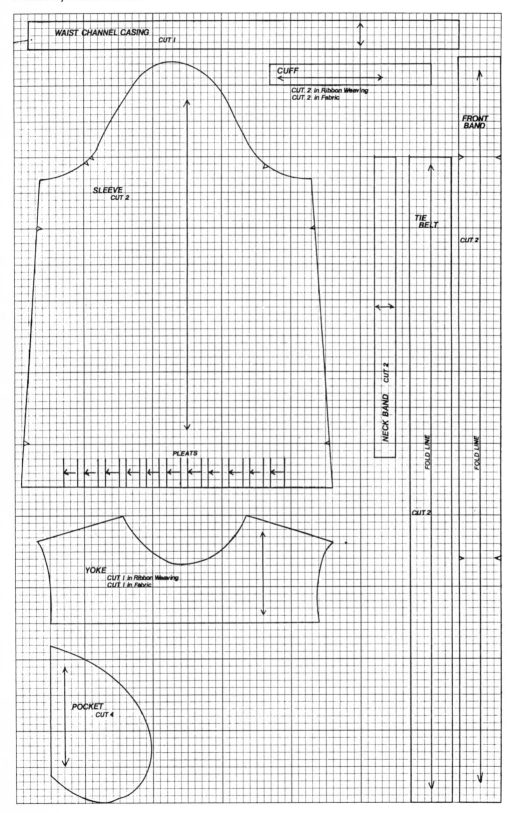

*Pattern for shirt dress.*

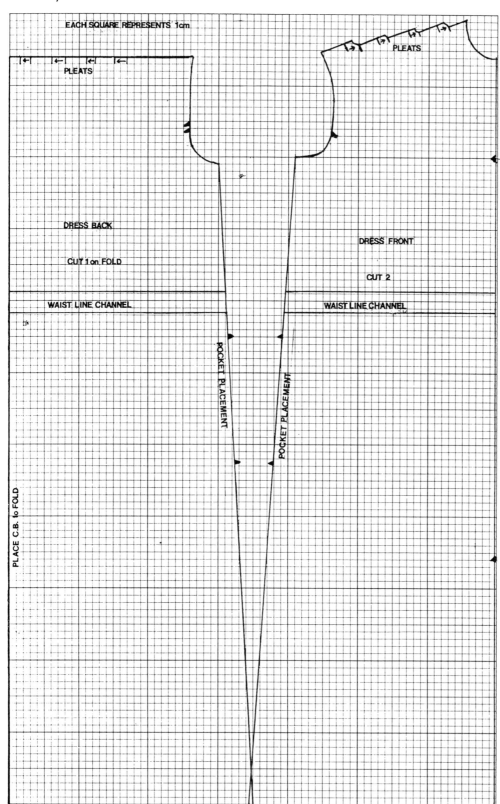

EACH SQUARE REPRESENTS 1cm

PLEATS

PLEATS

DRESS BACK

DRESS FRONT

CUT 1 on FOLD

CUT 2

WAIST LINE CHANNEL

WAIST LINE CHANNEL

POCKET PLACEMENT

POCKET PLACEMENT

PLACE C.B. to FOLD

## Making up

**1** Make pleats in the front and back bodice; tack in position.

### Yoke

**2** Place the right side of the ribbon yoke to the right side of the back bodice and machine in place.

**3** Place the right side of the back yoke facing to the wrong side of the back bodice and machine in place, stitching from the ribbon yoke and following previous row of machining. Trim the seams to 1cm (⅜in). Press the stitching and press seams up into the yoke.

**4** Pin and tack the front sections to the ribbon yoke, machine in place. Trim the seams to 1cm (⅜in) and press them up. Turn under the seam allowance on the yoke facing, tack and press; hand sew it in place (*fig. 1*).

**5** Place the pocket sections in between the balance marks and machine them in place. Press the seam towards the pocket.

**6** Pin, tack and machine the side seams together, stitching around the pocket. Neaten seams, press them open. Press the pocket towards the front (*fig. 2*).

**7** Press the interfacing on to the front band. Fold in half lengthways and press.

### Front bands

**8** Make a 3cm (1¼in) hem on the dress fronts and front band; check the fit.

**9** Place the right side of front band to the wrong side of both dress fronts. Machine in position. Press the stitching, trim the seam and press it towards the front band. Turn in the seam allowance along the edge of the front band and tack it in place onto the right side of both dress fronts (*fig. 3*).

**10** Top stitch the band close to the edge and again 6mm (¼in) away from the first row of stitching (*fig. 4*).

### Stand collar

**11** Press the interfacing to both sections of the collar.

**12** Turn under the seam allowance along one collar section. Tack, press and trim the seam allowance.

**13** Pin, tack and machine sections together on three sides, leaving open the notched edge. Trim, turn and press (*fig. 5*).

**14** Pin the collar to the wrong side of the neck, matching notches at shoulder, clipping the neck where necessary. Tack, machine and trim. Press the seam towards the collar.

**15** Tack the basted edge of the collar over the seam on the right side of the neck edge (*fig. 6*).

**16** Top stitch the collar with two rows of machining along the edge and again 6mm (¼in) in from the first row of machining.

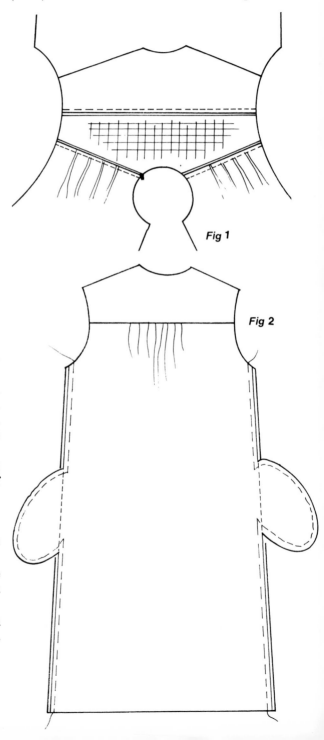

Fig 1

Fig 2

## Sleeve and cuff

**17** Make tucks in the lower edge of the sleeve on the inside by bringing the lines together, tack in place and machine to a depth of 4cm (1½in). Press towards the back of the sleeve (*fig. 7*).

**18** Stitch the sleeve seam, leaving it open below the lower notch. Neaten the seam and press open (*fig. 8*).

**19** Turn in the open edges along seam lines 6mm (¼in) on the raw edges, taper to nothing above the notch.

**20** Turn in the seam allowance along one edge of the cuff.

**21** Pin, tack and machine the cuff sections together at the upper edge and both ends. Trim, turn and press (*fig. 9*).

49
*Working drawings for shirt dress (figures 1-11).*

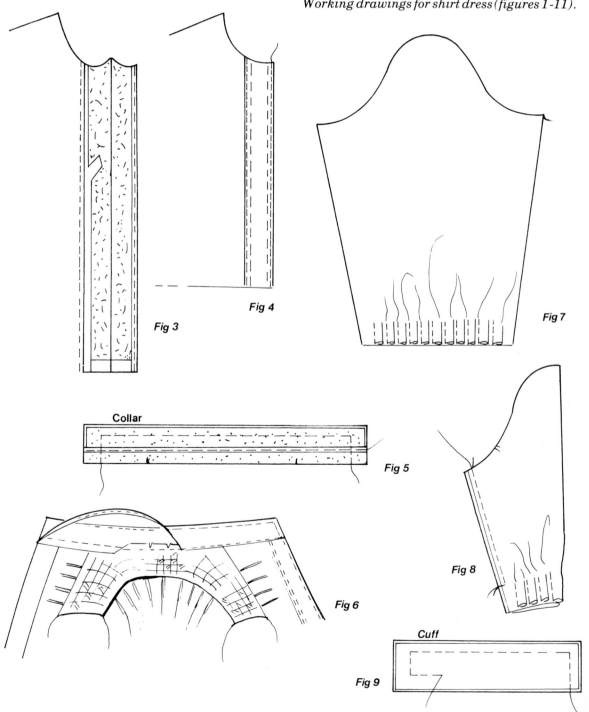

Fig 3

Fig 4

Collar

Fig 5

Fig 6

Fig 7

Fig 8

Cuff

Fig 9

**22** Pin the ribbon side of the cuff to the right side of the sleeve. Tack and machine in place. Trim and press the seam towards the cuff.

**23** Use one width of ribbon as your seam allowance and machine from the interfacing on the ribbon; this will enable you to see and machine accurately, leaving the cuff the width of three ribbons.

**24** Slip stitch the basted edge of the cuff on the inside over the seam (*fig. 10*).

**25** Pin the sleeve into the armhole. Adjust the ease and stitch it into position. Stitch again 6mm (¼in) away. Trim the seam to 1cm (⅜in). Neaten the seam. Turn the seam towards the sleeve.

*Casing*
**26** Make a buttonhole at each side of front band on the waistline, to bring the belt through the casing (*fig. 11*).

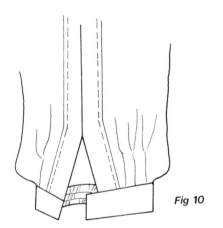

Fig 10

**27** To make the waistline casing, turn in 6mm (¼in) seam allowance along the length of the casing and centre the strip along placement lines, turning in the ends 13mm (½in); stitch close to the upper and lower edges, hand-stitch the ends in place.

*Hem*
**28** Level the hem and turn up to 3cm (1¼in). Neaten the edge. Tack and press. It can be finished by hand or, as this one has been, with a double row of machining 6mm (¼in) apart.

*Finishing*
**29** Make up the belt by machining the sections together along centre back. Fold in half lengthways and machine along the length of the belt and both ends, leaving a section to turn the belt through. Trim, turn and press.

**30** Topstitch with a double row of machining, starting and finishing at the centre back.

**31** Thread the belt through the waistline casing with a bodkin.

**32** Cover the buttons.

**33** Make machine buttonholes in the front band, lengthways and across at the neck edge, about 6cm (2½in) apart.

**34** Mark the position of buttons through the buttonholes and hand-sew in place.

**35** Use the small nylon snap fastener for the cuff closure, as buttonholes will make the ribbon fray.

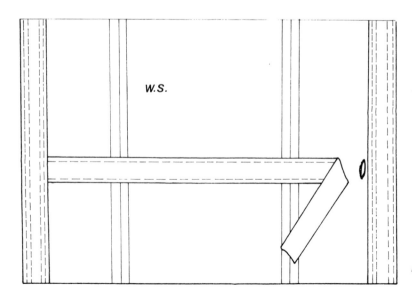

W.S.

Fig 11

50
*Illustration for shirt dress.*

# Travel coat

The travel coat (*colour plates 16 and 17*) is made in a quality waffle cotton and is designed to take apart, i.e. lower sleeves and lower skirt, collar and epaulets are all detachable using the poppa stud fasteners. The epaulets are woven with fabric and ribbon, the fabric for the epaulet being cut on the bias grain and trimmed with a bias strip. When all the detachable parts are removed, you have a jaunty fingertip-length jacket with a three-quarter length sleeve. The pattern for the long-sleeved velvet jacket is in fact the upper part of the travel coat.

Using any kind of stud fastener requires an interfacing directly beneath the stud to give stability to the fabric and prevent the fastener from being torn out of the garment. Make sure you fit them accurately by marking the position in the top part of your garment first and then, through this fitting hole, mark your base stud. This failsafe tip will ensure accurate positioning of top and base everytime. Continue by fitting your top studs first and then fit you base studs.

## Fitting the studs

The poppa studs used for the travel coat are in four parts; two parts for the top and two parts for the base. Place the top section of the stud into the disc and, with the wrong side of your garment facing you, place the hole in the garment over the stud (*fig. 1*). Press part (b) onto part (a) and using the assembling tool and hammer hit firmly once or twice until firmly together.

### To fit base

Place part (d) into the disc and with the right side of the garment facing you (*fig. 2*) place the hole in the coat over the stud. Place part (c) onto part (d) and with the B side of the assembling tool, hammer firmly into place. There should be no movement when these studs are in place.

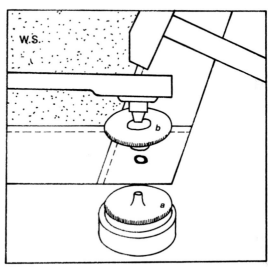

W.S.

**Fig. 1**

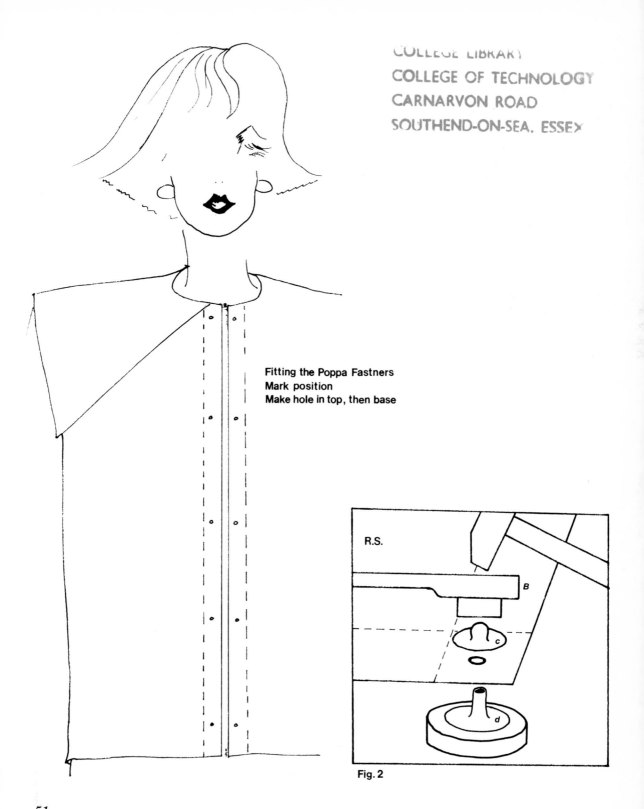

**Fitting the Poppa Fastners**
**Mark position**
**Make hole in top, then base**

R.S.

B

c

d

**Fig. 2**

*51*
*Fixing the studs for travel coat.*

## Evening purse with optional plaited shoulder strap

This plain-weave purse (*colour plate 15*) is very simple to weave and easy to make. It will look equally good in soft pastel colours or strong contrasts, or simply with ribbon of one colour.

The single-faced satin ribbon was used here, but the polyester grosgrain ribbon looks equally good and, since it is very hard-wearing proves ideal for purses.

### Materials
22 metres (25¼yd) of 10mm-wide navy blue ribbon.
2 metres 20cm (2½yd) of 3mm-wide burgundy ribbon.

*Plaited strap:*
2 metres 40cm (2¾yd) of 3mm-wide navy blue ribbon.
1 metre 20cm (1¼yd) of 3mm-wide burgundy ribbon.
Iron-on interfacing 29cm x 44cm (11½ x 17½in)
Canvas piece 25cm x 39cm (10in x 15½in)
Lining fabric 25cm x 39cm (10in x 15½in)
Matching sewing thread and glass headed pins.
Two Velcro spot-ons in a matching colour.

The measurements given allow for two 10mm ribbons to be turned in on all four sides as your seam allowance.

### Preparation
For warp ribbons, cut 26 lengths of 10mm-wide navy ribbon, 44cm (17½in) long, and 3 lengths of 3mm-wide burgundy ribbon, 44cm (17½in) long.

For weft ribbons, cut 33 lengths of 10mm-wide navy ribbon, 29cm (11½in) long, and 6 lengths of 3mm-wide burgundy ribbon, 29cm (11½in) long.

*Warp ribbon*
Follow the design layout in figure 52 starting from your top right-hand corner, pin down six navy ribbons: one burgundy, one navy, one burgundy, one navy, one burgundy. Pin out a further 18 navy ribbons to complete the warp.

*Weft ribbon*
Again working from your top right-hand corner and weaving in plain weave, work three rows of navy ribbon, * one of burgundy, one navy, one burgundy, one navy, one burgundy. ** Weave 23 more rows in navy ribbon. Then repeat from * to **, finishing off with a further three rows of navy ribbon. Press carefully and machine 6mm (¼in) in from the edge to hold ribbons in place.

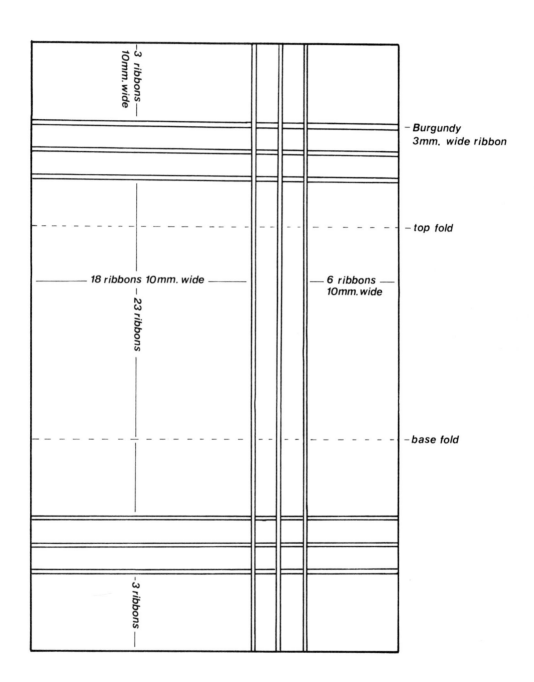

3 ribbons 10mm. wide

Burgundy 3mm. wide ribbon

top fold

18 ribbons 10mm. wide

6 ribbons 10mm. wide

23 ribbons

base fold

3 ribbons

52
*Design layout for evening purse.*

canvas

fig.1

fig. 2

lining

fig. 3

53
*Working drawings for evening purse (figures 1-4).*

fig. 4

90

**Making up the purse**

Place the canvas on to the wrong side of the ribbons and fold two ribbon widths over the canvas on all four sides as your seam allowance (fig. 1). Hand-sew in place.

*Plaited strap*

Using the 3mm-wide ribbon, two navy and one burgundy 1 metre 20cm (1¼yds) in length, make a three-strand plait. Begin by pinning all three ribbons firmly together on your board, and then plaiting them loosely together (fig. 2). Machine across both ends of the plait to hold the ribbons in place. Check the length of the strap for wearing purposes. Mark the position of the strap, 9cm (3½in) in from the edge along the top flap fold line, and stitch it firmly in place by hand (fig. 1).

*Lining*

Turn in the seam allowance on the lining and press. Place it over the canvas so that one ribbon is now showing on all four sides (*fig. 3*). Hand-sew it in place. Fold the purse along the lower fold line and hand-sew the side seams together with a small overhand stitch.

Fasten purse with velcro spot-ons, placing one section in each corner of the flap and one in each corner of the base to match (*fig. 4*).

## Black and white evening purse

Another idea for purse design is illustrated here. This black and white evening purse is made with 15mm-wide polyester grosgrain and satin ribbon. It is woven in plain weave, and fused to a heavyweight interfacing. It is lined throughout. A folded black satin ribbon was used to edge the purse and stitched in place with a small zig-zag stitch.

Velcro was used for the closure, and a small ribbon rose was made to decorate the purse.

*54*
*Black and white evening purse.*

# Ribbon belt with rivet trim

The grosgrain ribbon used to decorate this belt is a very simple and economical way of using ribbon as a trimming.

To calculate your belt length:

## Buckle belt

Measure your waist and add 3cm (1¼in) for the buckle, plus 15cm (6in) for the extension.

## Concealed overlap

Waist measurement plus 10cm (4in) for overlap.

## Materials

Belt backing or petersham (to fit buckle if used).
Backing fabric.
1 metre 12cm (1¼yd) each of 15mm-wide polyester grosgrain ribbon in red and black.
2 metres 24cm (2½yd) of white 3mm-wide double-faced satin ribbon.
1 packet of rivets (plus buckle or Velcro for closure).

## Method

**1** Machine the white ribbon down the centre of the black and red ribbon with a small zig zag stitch (*fig. 1*). Cut the ribbons into 14cm (5½in) lengths.

**2** Place the interfacing on the wrong side of fabric and tack it into place (*fig. 2*).

**3** Mark the backing fabric into 'V' shapes along the length of the belt.

**4** With the right side of the fabric facing you, place the ribbons in position and edge stitch in place (through interfacing), remove tacks and press (*fig. 3*). (The interfaced section is the right side of the belt, the other section is backing.)

**5** Turn the raw edges over the interfacing across both ends and along the upper and lower edges. Tack in place and press. Hand-sew in position. Remove and tacks and press again. (*fig. 4*).

55
*Ribbon belt with rivet trim.*

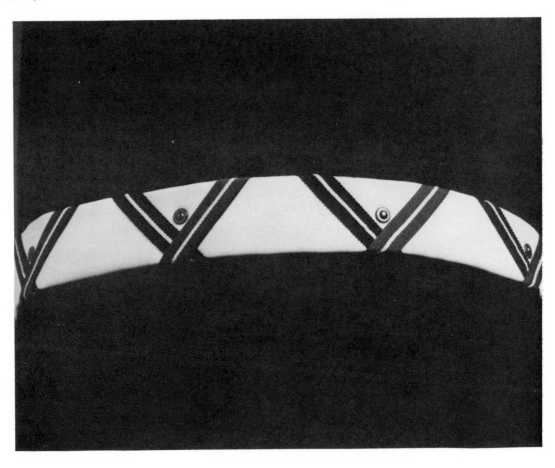

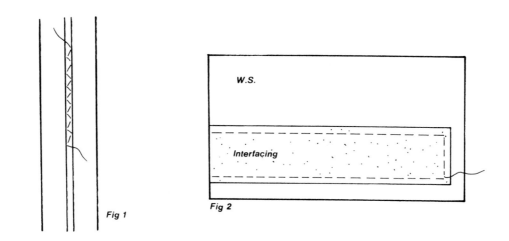

W.S.

Interfacing

Fig 1

Fig 2

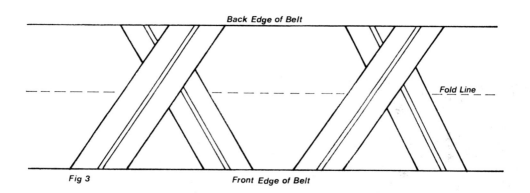

Back Edge of Belt

Fold Line

Fig 3

Front Edge of Belt

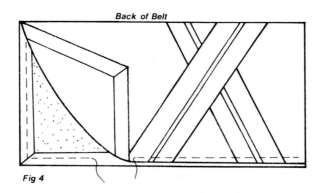

Back of Belt

Fig 4

56
*Ribbon belt working drawings (figures 1-6).*

**6** For the concealed overlap closure, fasten the belt, marking the overlap position, and place a 7cm (3in) x 3cm (1¼in) section of Velcro in place behind this mark, so that it is invisible from the right side of the belt. If a buckle is preferred, place the eyelet in the centre of the belt 3cm (1¼in) in from the edge and thread the belt through the buckle, insert the prong through the eyelet and fold back to the wrong side of the belt; hand sew in place. Check the fit of the belt and mark the position of the eyelet.

**7** Make three more eyelet holes, one 4cm (1½in) behind the first position and two more at 4cm (1½in) intervals towards the front overlap. Rivets were also added to decorate the belt.

*To fix rivets*
**8** Mark the spot where rivets are to be placed (*fig. 5*).

**9** Make a hole in the belt with the assembling tool and hammer.

**10** Place the base of the rivet in the disc (*fig. 6*) and with the right side of the belt facing you, position the hole in the belt over the base. Place the rivet in position over the base and use the assembling tool and hammer to close.

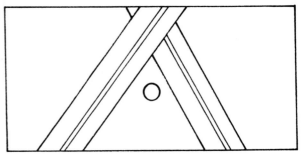

Fig 5    Mark Position for Rivets

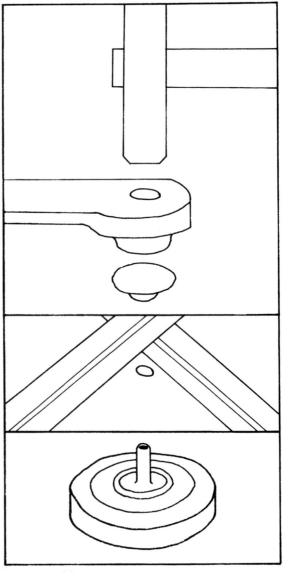

Fig 6    Fixing the Rivets

# Patchwork quilt and pillow set

This lovely quilt (*colour plates 18 and 19*) could become a family heirloom. It is simple to make and not too time consuming, although it is quite extravagant with ribbons and lace. Nevertheless, we had a lot of fun working it all out and a lot of satisfaction seeing it complete.

Three different coloured ribbons were used in the weaving of the squares, and a fourth ribbon, with picot edge, was used to trim the patchwork and lace edging.

*57*
*Bed quilt working sketch.*

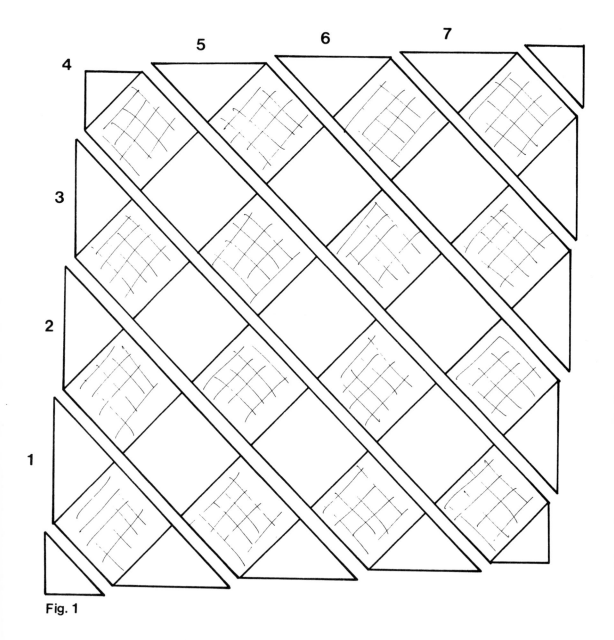

Fig. 1

*BED QUILT –* *Cut fabric into squares of 25cm each*
*plus* **16** *ribbon squares of 25cm each*

## Materials

5 metres (5½yd) of 112cm (44in)-wide cotton polyester fabric for the quilt plus 1 metre (1¼yd) for the pillow.

*Each square uses:*
4 metres (4½yd) of 13mm-wide (½in) dark pink single-faced satin ribbon.
4 metres 25cm (4¾yd) of 10mm-wide (⅜in) pale pink single-faced satin ribbon.
3 metres 50cm (4yd) of 7mm-wide (¼in) jacquard ribbon.
3 metres 25cm (4yd) of 10mm-wide (⅜in) pale pink picot-edge ribbon for applique.
1 metre 50cm (1¾yd) ultrasoft iron-on interfacing for ribbon weaving.
1 metre 50cm (1¾yd) x 137cm (54in) polyester wadding (optional).

All measurements are for a standard double bed. You would need only half this amount of ribbon for a single bed, or more for a king-size bed.

## Preparation

*Each patchwork of ribbon*
A 1cm (⅜in) seam allowance is allowed in measurements on both fabric and ribbon. When sewn together, each square in the quilt will measure 23cm (9in) square.

1 Cut the ribbon into 25cm (10in) lengths: each square uses 17 lengths of pale pink, 13 lengths of jacquard and 15 lengths of dark pink ribbon, woven in that order.

2 Cut the fabric into 17 squares, 25cm (10in) square. Cut 7 of these squares in half diagonally, making 14 triangles.

3 Cut 16 squares of interfacing 26cm (10¼in) square (you will find it easier to work the weaving if interfacing is slightly larger than ribbon), trim away the excess interfacing when weaving is complete.

*Weaving*
Weave 16 squares of ribbon using the plain weave described on page 14, following the sequence above. Each square takes roughly three quarters of an hour to weave.

*Making up*
1 Using figure 1 as your guide, join the ribbon and fabric squares alternately together. With right sides together, pin and machine them in place and press, making up one strip at a time. Number each strip as you work.

2 With your numbers in sequence and with right sides together, pin and machine each strip in place until the quilt top is complete. Press each strip as you work.

3 Cover all seams with the 10mm picot-edge ribbon.

*Backing* (optional)
4 If you are using a polyester wadding, place this over the back of the work and baste them together around the edge.

*Side – top – base section*
5 Cut one section of fabric for the base = 209cm x 41cm (82in x 16in).

6 Cut two sections of fabric for the sides = 132cm x 41cm (52in x 16in).

7 Cut one section of fabric for the top = 209cm x 60cm (82in x 24in).

8 With right sides together, pin and machine the side panels in place (*fig. 2*). Press towards hem.

9 Fit the base and top sections in place, following the diagram in figure 2.

*Hem and lace finish*
10 Make a narrow hem around the edge. The quilt can now be left plain, if you wish, or finish with gathered lace and ribbon for a glamorous look, as on this one. The lace and ribbon around the top and hem are held in place with a small zig-zag stitch over a 5mm-wide ribbon.

A vallance was made for the bed in matching waffle fabric.

*20. Apricot and cream table setting woven with fabric and ribbon.*

21. Detail of table mat woven with fabric and ribbon.

22. Ribbon rose picture. (Ann Olphin).

# BED QUILT

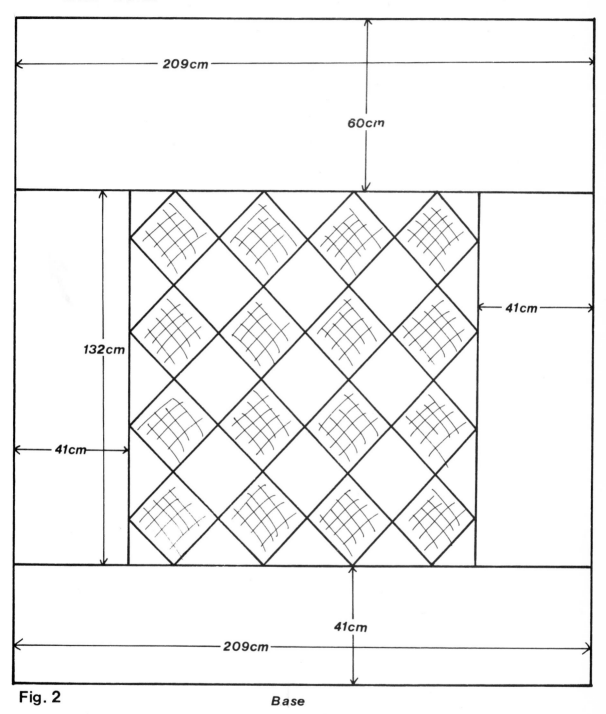

Fig. 2                                    Base

*58*
*Bed quilt illustration.*

## Pillows

The centre piece for the pillows and cushion were made with the fabric cut on the straight grain and woven in the bias weave. Follow the instructions given on page 21 and weave a section measuring 28cm x 25cm (11in x 9¾in).

### Materials
Cut one pillow section 48cm x 92cm (19in x 36in) (this includes your 18cm (7in) turn-back section).

Cut one section 74cm x 48cm (29in x 19in) for backing pillow.

### Making-up
1 Place the woven section of pillow 23cm (9in) in from the left-hand edge (*fig. 3*) and top stitch in place. Cover the raw edges of the centre panel

with gathered lace and 5mm-wide ribbon. Machine in place with a small zig-zag stitch.

2 To decorate the edge of the pillow, measure 4cm (1½in) in from pillow edges and machine lace and ribbon in place.

3 With right sides together and keeping the lace away from the edge, pin the back section to front section, fold the overlap over the top of the back section to sandwich them together. Stitch 1cm (⅜in) in from the edge on three sides, trim the corner, turn to the right side and press carefully.

The lace trimming on the bed quilt and pillows was dyed with cold tea to obtain this antique look, as the colour proved impossible to find. To dye your own lace simply make a pot of tea using three tea bags, leave for about ten minutes to infuse, the remove tea bags, pour tea in a glass basin and submerge the lace for five minutes. Rinse in lots of cold water until water is clear, then dry the lace and use in the normal way.

*59*
*Pillow case working sketches.*

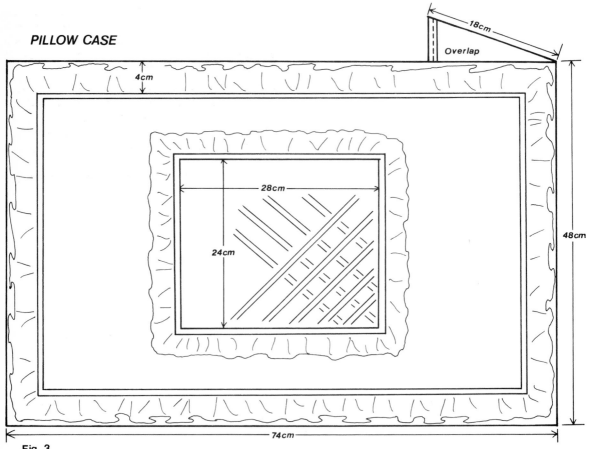

Fig. 3

98

# Table setting

This lovely table setting (*colour plates 20 and 21*), made in a toning colour combination of apricot and cream, was very economical to make as the fabric is cut on the straight grain. Weaving fabric and ribbon together produces a very exciting texture, and used here for the table mats makes them very practical as they are slightly padded and easily laundered, being made in a polyester and cotton mixture. This combination of fabric and ribbon gives a really luxurious look to any garment and looks interesting woven in contrasting or toning shades of ribbon, depending on the look you are trying to achieve.

## *Table mats*

### Materials
The finished size of one table mat is 28cm x 41cm (11in x 16¼in).
For one mat you will need: 65cm (¾yd) of apricot polyester cotton fabric 115cm (45in) wide.
8 metres (8¾yd) of 10mm single-faced satin cream ribbon.
1 metre 50cm (1¾yd) of lace trimming.
30cm (½yd) of lightweight iron-on interfacing.
Trimming and tape maker 25mm.

### Method
**1** Cut the interfacing to 43cm x 30cm (12in x 17in) [this includes a 1cm (⅜in) seam allowance all round].

**2** Cut one piece of apricot fabric to 43cm x 30cm (17in x 12in) for the backing.

**3** Cut six strips of apricot fabric 5cm (2in) wide (each table mat uses six strips of fabric, cut across the width of the fabric).

**4** Following the directions given on page 21, weave the fabric and ribbon in the bias design for the table mats. When complete, press well and machine 6mm (¼in) in from the edge to hold the weaving in place.

**5** Place the fabric backing over the weaving, right sides together, and machine 1cm (⅜in) in from the edge on three sides, leaving a 12cm (4½in) opening on the fourth side. Trim seams, clip corners, turn to the right side and press (*fig. 1*).

**6** Close the opening by hand-sewing the edges together.

*60*
*Table setting working sketches (figues 1-4).*

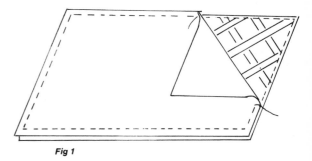

**Fig 1**

*Lace trimming*

**7** Hand-sew the lace in the place (*fig. 2*) 6mm (¼in) in from the edge and folding the lace at the corner to give the appearance of a mitred corner (*fig. 4*).

## Napkins

### Materials

50cm (20in) of 115cm (45in) wide apricot polyester cotton (makes two napkins).
4 metres (4½yd) of picot-edge 6mm (¼in) wide cream polyester satin ribbon.

### Method

**1** Cut the apricot fabric into two pieces 50cm x 50cm (20in x 20in).

**2** Make a single hem 6mm (¼in) deep on to right side of fabric and press in place.

**3** Place the picot-edge ribbon over this raw edge, so that the fancy edge of the ribbon is also showing over the edge of the napkin. Machine in place with a small zig-zag stitch, and press (*fig. 3*).

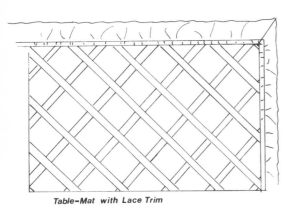

Table-Mat with Lace Trim

Fig 2

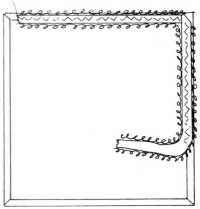

Fig 3

Napkin trimmed with Picot edge ribbon

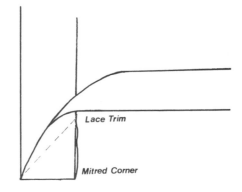

Lace Trim

Fig 4

Mitred Corner

## Quilted tea cosy and egg cosy

Finished size 30cm x 25cm (12in x 10in).

The tea cosy and egg cosy are simple projects for any one to try and are made in wadded quilting, also known as English quilting, consisting of three layers of fabric held together by top stitching over the narrow ribbon to give surface texture and keep in the warmth.

Tea cosy 30cm x 25cm (12in x 10in).
Egg cosy 10½cm x 11½cm (4¼ x 4½in).

*61*
*Tea cosy and egg cosy pattern.*

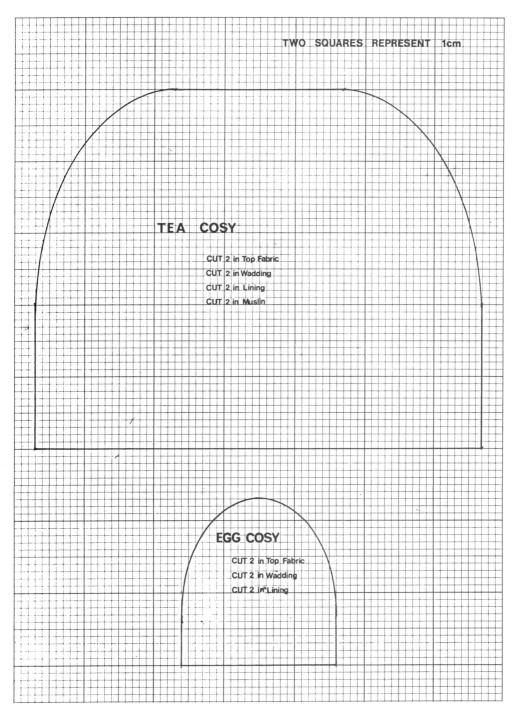

TWO SQUARES REPRESENT 1cm

**TEA COSY**

CUT 2 in Top Fabric
CUT 2 in Wadding
CUT 2 in Lining
CUT 2 in Muslin

**EGG COSY**

CUT 2 in Top Fabric
CUT 2 in Wadding
CUT 2 in Lining

## Materials

30cm of 90cm wide (12in x 36in) cotton fabric will make one tea cosy and two egg cosies.

30cm of 90cm wide (12in x 36in) lining.

50cm (20in) piece of 4oz synthetic wadding (padding).

½ metre (½yd) of 90cm (36in) wide contrasting fabric for making bias trimming to trim both tea and egg cosies.

15 metres (16½yd) of 3mm polyester crepe ribbon in a contrasting colour for quilting both sides of tea cosy and egg cosy.

Matching sewing thread to ribbon.

50cm (19½in) of muslin.

Paper and pencil.

The instructions here are for the tea cosy, but the egg cosy is made in exactly the same way.

## Order of work

Enlarge pattern pieces (*two* squares represent 1cm = half scale) and add 1cm (½in) seam allowance on lower edges only; the curved edge is bound with a bias trim, so no extra seams allowance is necessary. Cut two pieces of top fabric, two pieces of wadding, two pieces of lining fabric and two pieces of muslin.

**1** Press all the fabrics thoroughly before you start your quilting.

**2** Mark the first diagonal line in each direction on the top fabric, using a dressmaker's water-erasable pen and ruler (*fig. 1*). The parallel lines either side will be 3cm (1¼in) apart and can be marked at this stage with the pen, or by using the gauge or edge-marker attached to your quilting foot on the machine after the first row of quilting is in place.

**3** Place the wadding over the muslin and place the top fabric, right side facing you, over the wadding.

**4** Tack all layers together, thoroughly smoothing the fabric as you tack from the centre outwards all over the tea cosy.

## Prepare your machine

Fit the embroidery foot onto the machine. Set the machine to a wide zig-zag stitch, the width of the ribbon. Thread your machine with a thread to match your ribbon.

## Machining the quilting

Place the tea cosy with the right side facing you under the presser foot with the narrow ribbon under the centre of the foot and machine along the longest diagonal line first. Smooth the fabric out with your hands to keep it taut as you machine across to the end of the row. Work all the rows of machining in the same direction to prevent the fabric pulling in opposite directions, which will cause puckering. Work either side of the first line 3cm (1¼in) apart until the tea cosy is covered in one direction. Turn the work around and machine again on the longest diagonal line and complete the diamond patern by working either side of this line until the work is complete. If both sides are quilted, repeat for the second half.

## Making up the tea cosy

With right sides together, place linings on top of the quilting sections and trim the linings to fit. Pin, tack and machine together across the bottom edge only. Trim wadding away, layer seams and press very carefully on the lining (*fig. 2*). Place front and back of sections together, right sides out and linings together. Pin and tack through all layers. Machine front and back together 1cm (½in) in from the edge. Trim raw edges. Make a small loop with 8cm (3⅛in) of ribbon and sew in the centre of the top edge (*fig. 3*).

## Binding

Press cut edges of bias strip to meet at the centre, reducing the width to 2.5cm (1in). Fold in half lengthways so that one edge is slightly shorter than the underside. Press well. Bind the edge of the tea cosy. Pin, tack and topstitch in place (*fig. 4*).

*62*
*Tea cosy working pattern (figures 1-4).*

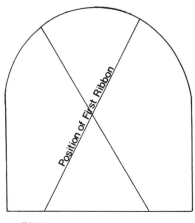

FiG 1

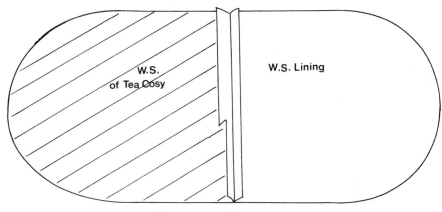

W.S.
of Tea Cosy

W.S. Lining

Fig 2

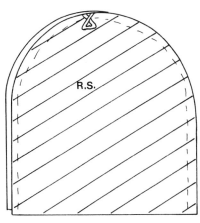

R.S.

Fig 3

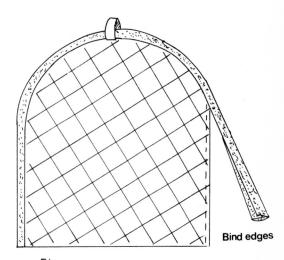

Bind edges

Fig 4

# Cube-weave cushion

A beautifully-made cushion just adds the finishing touches needed to make a room look complete. Working the cube-weave design with the exquisite Swiss jacquard ribbon gives this cushion (*colour plate 4*) a look of richness in the patchwork effect. Choose one colour in the design to blend with your furnishing and then choose a contrast that will echo the other colours in the room.

## Material

(To make a cushion 41cm (16in) square.)
5 metres (5½yd) of 35mm (1½in) white nylon velvet ribbon.
5 metres (5½yd) of 35mm (1½in) green nylon velvet ribbon.
5 metres (5½yd) of 35mm (1½in) Swiss-woven jacquard.
A piece of lightweight interfacing 44cm (17in) square.
50cm (½yd) of 90cm (36in) wide lining (backing).
2 metres (2yd) of piping cord.
Glass-headed pins.
20cm (8in) zip.

Following the instructions given on page 19, make up the woven panel and proceed as follows.

## Cutting out

Trim the woven section to measure approximately 44cm (17in) square.

Cut two lining (backing) sections measuring 23cm x 44cm (9in x 17in). Cut bias strips (*fig. 1*) 3cm (1¼in) wide and sew them together until you have approximately 1 metre 80cm (2yd) in length of bias trimming (*fig. 2*).

## To make the cushion

1 Fold the bias trimming around the cord and tack as close as possible to the cord (*fig. 3*).

2 Pin and tack piping around the seam allowance of the ribbon-woven section (*fig. 4*). Overlap the ends of the piping by trimming the cord to meet the first cord. Fold the fabric edge under 6mm (¼in). Wrap this folded edge over the piping, letting the cord ends meet (*fig. 5*). Machine the piping in position as close as possible to the cord.

3 With right sides together, pin and machine top and base of centre back sections to a depth of 11cm (4¾in). Press seams open (*fig. 6*). Tack the zip in place centrally over the seam and between the machine stitching. Machine all round the zip.

4 Open zip. With right sides facing, pin and tack the lining in place.

5 Machine in position by stitching with the wrong side of the ribbon weaving facing you, so that you are following the machine stitching for the piping as your guide.

6 Trim seams and clip corners. Turn to the right side through the open zip. Press carefully (*fig. 7*).

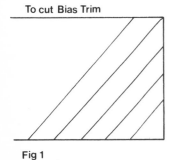

To cut Bias Trim

Fig 1

Fig 2

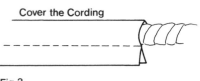

Cover the Cording

Fig 3

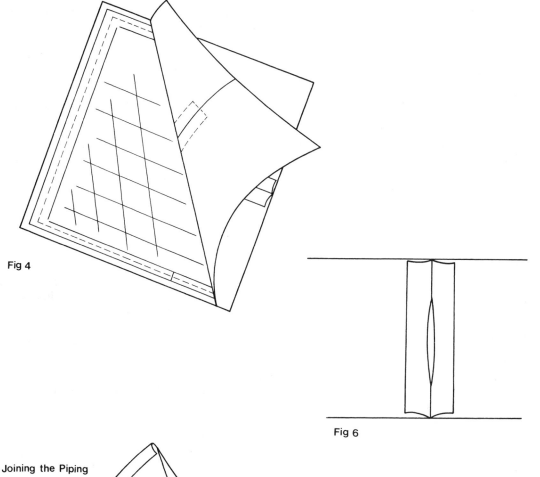

Fig 4

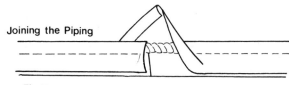

Joining the Piping

Fig 5

Fig 6

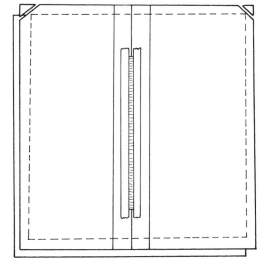

Fig 7

*63*
*Cushion.*

# Ribbon flowers

The design of this lovely ribbon picture (*colour plate 22*) can also be used to decorate your fashion garments, purses or cushions. Small clusters of ribbon flowers look beautiful on the shoulder of your dress or jacket and trailing down to the waistline; or simply scatter an evening dress or skirt all over, with perhaps a sequin in the centre to sparkle in the evening lights. Try making a small posy onto a velvet ribbon to wear around your neck, with beads stitched into the centre; or decorate a small comb and wear it in your hair.

## Ribbon rose picture

Materials
2 metres (2¼yd) of 13mm-wide single-faced satin ribbon for leaves.
3 metres (3¼yd) of 13mm-wide single-faced satin ribbon for roses.
1 metre (1yd) of 7mm-wide ribbon for twigs and small flowers.
A glazed box frame with light hardboard or heavy card backing.
Velvet to cover backing.
Glue: spray glue and impact adhesive.
Fine florists' silver wire.

## Method

*Small petal flowers*
**1** Cut 5cm (2in) of 7mm-wide ribbon and bend it in half.

**2** Sandwich the fine wire in between (*fig. 1*), right side outside, so that the wire is like a leaf vein. Glue together.

**3** Make five petals for each flower required. Shape each top by cutting along the dotted line. (*fig. 2*).

**4** The centre of the flower is a piece of wire bent like a hairpin and bound (*fig. 3*) with thin ribbon held in place by glue. Attach the petals one at a time to the centre, binding them on tightly with fine wire (*fig. 4*).

**5** Cut away the surplus at the back and bend petals into shape (*fig. 5*).

*Leaves*
**6** Fold the 13mm ribbon (*fig. 6*) and glue it, wrong sides together, with impact adhesive.

**7** Cut off the surplus ribbon to leave the leaf shape (*fig. 7*).

*Twigs*
**8** Smear impact adhesive down the florists' wire and twist ribbon along its full length. Glue each end of the ribbon.

**9** Bend the wire in half to form two twigs, curve slightly. For smaller twigs, cut into sections and curve.

*Ribbon rose*
**10** Holding the 13mm-wide ribbon in the right hand, fold the end of the ribbon back with the left hand, to form a diagonal line with the right side of the ribbon facing (*fig. 8*).

**11** Roll the ribbon backwards with the left hand to form a tight roll until all the diagonal line is used up (*fig. 9*). With the ribbon in the right hand, lift it and fold a little of the top over towards the front. Turn at the same time with the left hand towards the back. The centre, which was tight, now starts to spread out. Repeat three times (*fig. 10*).

**12** Place your right thumb over the centre of the rose bud and bend the ribbon backwards while turning. Continue until the desired size is reached (*fig. 11*).

Experiment with different designs by laying the flower and leaves on the backing. When you are satisfied with your composition, you are ready to make the picture.

Take your box frame. This can be of any size you like, but it must have a space of 2cm (¾in) between the glass and the backing. Use a spray glue to stick the velvet to the backboard. Stick your flowers, twigs and leaves into place using impact adhesive sparingly. Brush the velvet and clean the glass. Position the frame over the backing and glue together at the corners. Attach the hanging fittings.

*64*
*Ribbon flowers.*

**Petal Flowers**

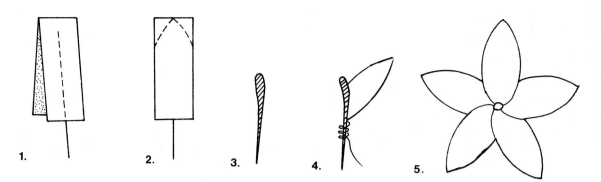

1.  2.  3.  4.  5.

**Leaves**

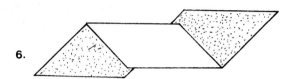

6.  7.

**Ribbon Rose**

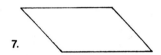

8.  9.

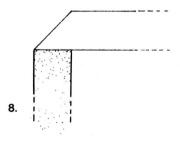

10.

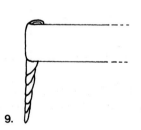

11.

# GENERAL HINTS

Keep your garment designs as simple as possible. Choose fabrics that have an interesting texture rather than a colourful print, as both the ribbon weaving and fabric weaving build areas of great richness and texture. Avoid weaving sections that require darts or seams for shaped areas, it is better to use the ribbon-weaving sections for collars, cuffs, yoke and inserts rather than an entire bodice. Although this can be done successfully, it is inclined to be a little bulky.

If you are in any doubt about your design and choice of fabric or ribbon, it would be a good idea to make a toile (mock-up) of your garment in an old sheet or calico. You could then pin a few of the ribbons in your chosen design, or mark in pencil the areas to be woven in ribbon, and see if you like the effect. You may decide at this stage to make the shoulder yoke deeper, for instance, so that more of the weaving is visible from the front. Your pattern could be altered accordingly by adding on to the front yoke section and by taking off the same amount on the front bodice line.

The garments in this book are quite simple and unstructured and not too difficult to make or fit and will suit most shapes and sizes. If, however, you prefer to use a good commercial pattern, whose fitting you can rely on, you could then adapt any of the weaving designs and combinations illustrations here to help you create your own texture and style by using your own thoughts for colour and fabric. Try also to weave a few samples in various colours and textures. Weaving the various designs illustrated here in small sections means you could make lots of samples in various colours and textures. When you shop for your fabrics, for instance, have these samples with you to place on to the fabric. This will show you immediately if this is the effect you are looking for and hopefully will inspire you to try out other ideas.

Bonding the ribbons together with an iron-on interfacing is very quick and time saving. Always use the very lightest weight, regardless of the weight of ribbon you weave, machining them in place immediately after cutting out the various sections.

# 4. Ribbons for Fashion:

## IDEAS FROM THE DESIGNER'S SKETCH PAD

The designs sketched here are ideas you can adapt yourself to use on your existing garments. For instance, the knitted jacket uses squares of satin ribbon for applique and small studs as an extra decoration. The navy blouse has a detachable panel of weaving in white with a large red bow at the neck, making a simple blouse look stunning.

The wedding dress bodice could be adapted from a readily available commercial pattern and would look sumptuous embellished with rhinestone and pearls.

The lavender two-piece could be altered from your own existing patterns by making it straight from the shoulder line and marking the position for the decorative panel at the chest and hip line. To get the balance correct, make the lower panel slightly deeper than the shoulder panel.

For the white angora jacket, simply trim the collar, hipband and cuffs with ribbons woven in plain weave, and for a really stunning and sophisticated look use black and white.

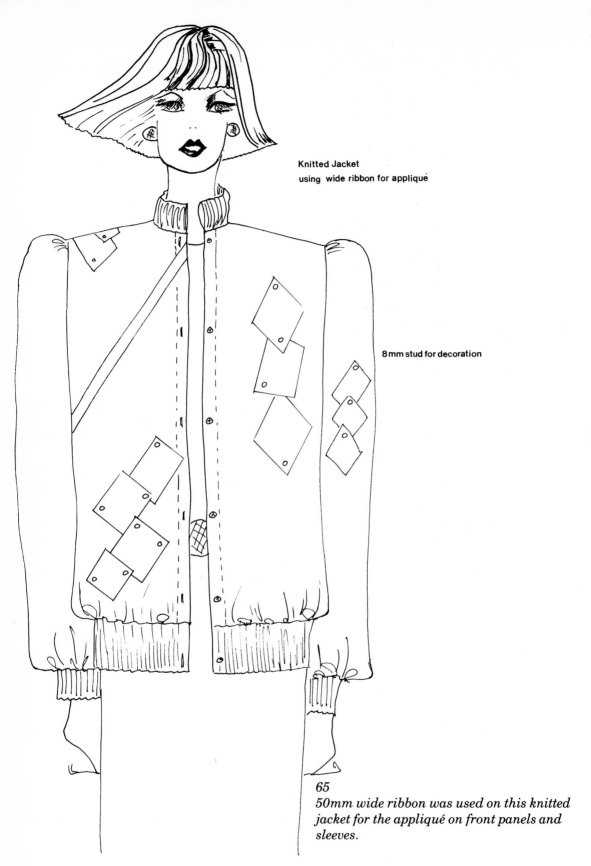

Knitted Jacket
using wide ribbon for appliqué

8mm stud for decoration

*65*
*50mm wide ribbon was used on this knitted*
*jacket for the appliqué on front panels and*
*sleeves.*

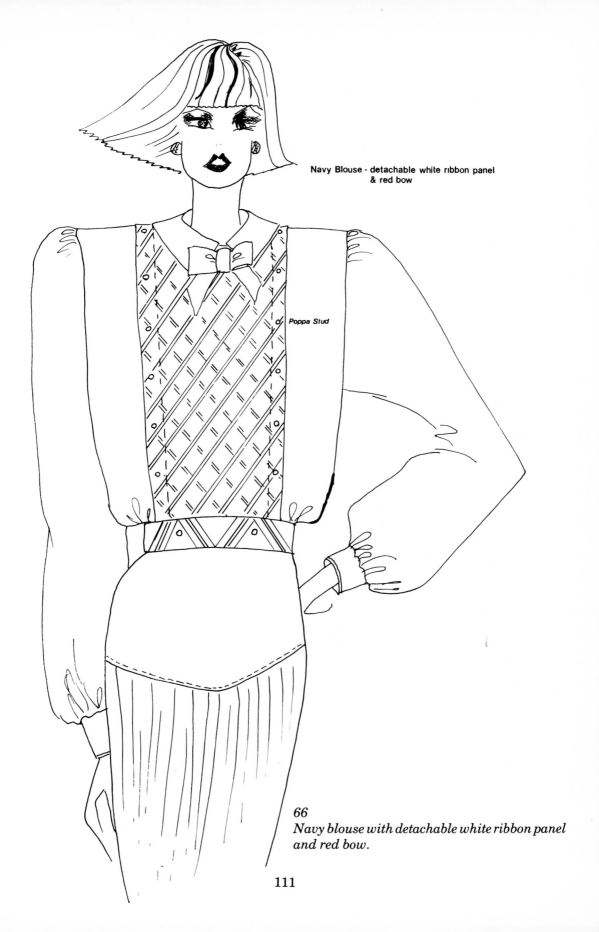

Navy Blouse - detachable white ribbon panel
& red bow

Poppa Stud

66
*Navy blouse with detachable white ribbon panel
and red bow.*

111

67
*This lovely wedding gown has fabric weaving on the bodice and is embellished with small pearls and sequins. The front and back yoke is made in fine net and the full sleeve and skirt with long train are made in a textured cream silk taffeta.*

112

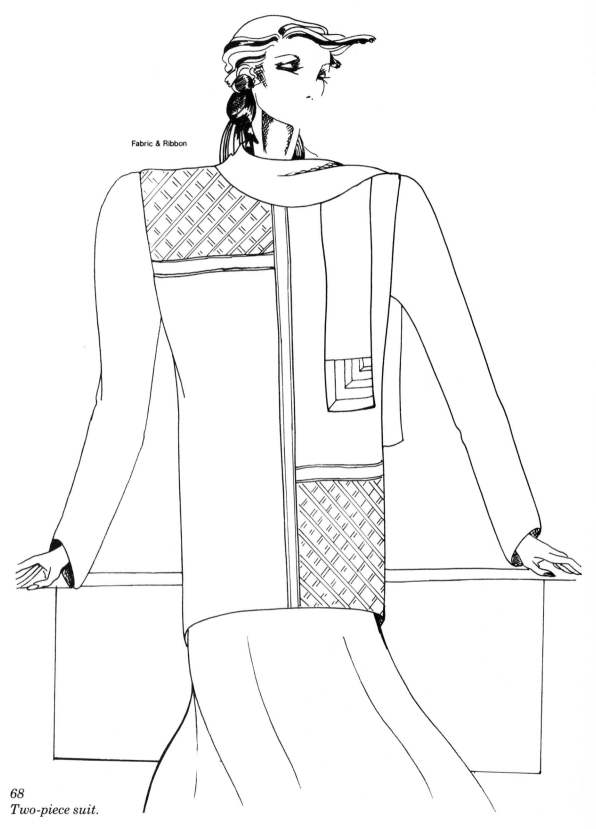

Fabric & Ribbon

*68*
*Two-piece suit.*

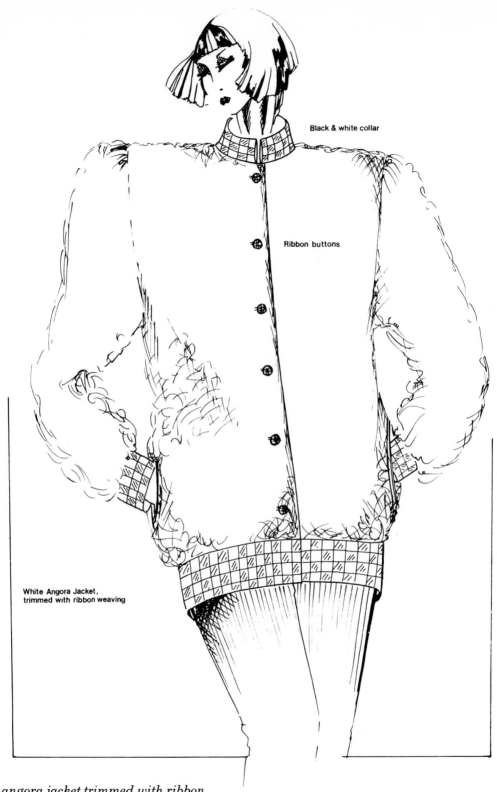

Black & white collar

Ribbon buttons

White Angora Jacket,
trimmed with ribbon weaving

*69*
*White angora jacket trimmed with ribbon*
*weaving.*

# LIST OF SUPPLIERS

Fabrics for the garments in this book were obtained from ordinary retail shops.

John Lewis Partnership Ltd., Oxford Street, London, W1A 1EX, and their many branches throughout the country, (for a wide selection of ribbons, interlinings, sewing accessories and fabrics).

McCullock & Wallis Ltd., 25/26 Dering Street, London, W1R 0BH, (for ribbons, Velcro, needles, pins, scissors, rouleau turner, tapemaker, poppa studs, rivets, iron-on interfacing and wadding).

Liberty & Company Ltd., Regent Street, London, W1R 6BA, (for a wide selection of sewing aids and fabrics).

Silkworm, 104 Warwick Street, Leamington Spa, Warwickshire, CV32 4QP.

Unicorn Fabrics, Woodstock, Oxford, (for sewing aids, ribbons and fabrics).

Beatties Ltd., 132 The Parade, Sutton Coldfield, (for sewing aids, ribbons and fabrics).

Scofields (Yorks.) Ltd., The Headrow, Leeds, LS1 6LS, (for a wide selection of ribbons, interlinings and sewing accessories).

# SEWING AIDS

*Product name:*

**U.K.**

Panda Ribbons

Velcro & Spot-ons

Rigilene

Poppa Studs

Rivets

Trimming & Tape Maker

Rouleau Turner

Vilene

**U.S.A.**

Panda Ribbons

Velcro & Spot-ons

Rigilene

Poppa Studs

Rivets

Trimming & Tape Maker

Rouleau Turner

Pellon

# BIBLIOGRAPHY

For further reading for students on the history of the ribbon weaving industry:

Ciba Review 24, *The Basle Ribbon Industry*, Basle, 1939.

Coventry in Crisis 1858-1863, Peter Searby, University of Warwick Open Studies: Coventry Historical Association, 1977.

*The Industrial Revolution in Coventry*, John Priest, Oxford University Press, 1960.

*Master & Artisan in Victorian England*, Evelyn, Adams & Mackay Ltd, 1969.

*Needlecraft*, Vol. nos. 22 and 63, first and second series, Manchester School of Embroidery, 1900.

# INDEX